coastal *kitchen*

Page 1: The black-sand Bethells Beach on Auckland's rugged west coast. Page 2: At Moeraki Beach, south of Oamaru, spherical boulders are scattered on the beach like a giant's marbles; some have eroded from shoreline bluffs. Page 3: Edged by its wild and beautiful beach and the Hokitika River, Hokitika township is at the centre of a West Coast area known for its rainforests and wetlands. Pages 4 and 5 (Contents): French Bay on Banks Peninsula is the idyllic outlook for the historic village of Akaroa, which began as a French settlement.

First published in 2008 by New Holland Publishers (NZ) Ltd
Auckland • Sydney • London • Cape Town

www.newhollandpublishers.co.nz

218 Lake Road, Northcote, Auckland 0627, New Zealand
Unit 1, 66 Gibbes Street, Chatswood, NSW 2067, Australia
86–88 Edgware Road, London W2 2EA, United Kingdom
80 McKenzie Street, Cape Town 8001, South Africa

ISBN: 978 1 86966 228 8

Commissioned by Belinda Cooke
Project managed by Louise Armstrong
General and regional introductions written by Glenda Kane
Captions written by Brian O'Flaherty
Edited by Sarah Elworthy
Designed by Christine Hansen
A catalogue record for this book is available from the National Library of New Zealand.
10 9 8 7 6 5 4 3 2 1

Colour reproduction by SC (Sang Choy) International Pte Ltd, Singapore
Printed by Craft Print Pte Ltd, on paper sourced from sustainable forests.

coastal *kitchen*

Photography by Ian Batchelor

Delicious food
from New Zealand's
seaside eateries

NEW
HOLLAND

Contents

Introduction

Kiwi chefs have long been in on the secret that fresh is best, that simple beats fussy, and that local can be world-dominating. They know it makes sense to cook and serve locally caught seafood the same day. They understand that selecting vegetables and fruit that were in the ground or on the tree this morning makes for better, tastier dishes.

Coastal Kitchen celebrates the sum of four parts: the sea, the land, the food and the chefs whose creativity sparkles from these shores. Award-winning photographer Ian Batchelor has travelled the length of New Zealand to beautifully capture a country, a coastline and a cuisine. From kumara and kiwifruit in the north to crayfish and oysters in the south, from pale sand beaches in the east to dramatic dark stretches on the west, many will be inspired to follow in his footsteps, seeking fabulous food and superb scenery in equal measure.

The restaurants and cafés featured in this cookbook represent the cream of the coastal crop. They hug the hills, perch on disused jetties, nestle into pockets of serene native bush or sit proudly on cliff tops, ensuring patrons are immersed in the inspiring landscape as they eat.

Regional and seasonal specialties have stood the test of time to earn their place in these pages, although there are also hints of many other cuisines and culinary practices. After all, it is in Kiwis' DNA to travel, and when they do, they return with fresh ideas and influences from around the globe. Geographically young and exciting, this country thrives on innovation.

In New Zealand it is impossible to be far from the sea, and even inland there is a distinct smell of salt on the breeze. With a coastline of more than 15,000 km, everyone in search of tranquility – or adventure – can secure their own secret spot.

For domestic chefs, standing at their kitchen bench seeking a departure from the everyday, and even for those who wish simply to feast with their eyes *Coastal Kitchen* is a window to another world – one of beauty, creativity and inspiration.

The magnificent surf beach at Mount Maunganui in the sunny Bay of Plenty is a popular summer playground.

NEW ZEALAND

Tasman Sea

South Pacific Ocean

NORTH ISLAND

- Maitai Bay
- *Bay of Islands*
- Waitangi
- Russell
- Paihia
- *Hokianga Harbour*
- Omapere
- **NORTHLAND**
- *Hauraki Gulf*
- *Coromandel Peninsula*
- Waiheke Is.
- Whitianga
- Flaxmill Bay
- Hahei
- Hot Water Beach
- **AUCKLAND**
- **TAURANGA**
- Mt Maunganui
- **BAY OF PLENTY**
- *East Cape*
- **EAST COAST**
- Tolaga Bay
- **GISBORNE**
- **NEW PLYMOUTH**
- **TARANAKI**
- **HAWKE'S BAY**
- **NAPIER**
- Te Awanga

SOUTH ISLAND

- *Golden Bay*
- Pohara Beach
- Mapua
- Havelock
- Queen Charlotte Sound
- **NELSON**
- Picton
- **WELLINGTON**
- **MARLBOROUGH**
- Barrytown
- Kaikoura
- Hokitika
- **WEST COAST**
- **CHRISTCHURCH**
- **CANTERBURY**
- Akaroa
- *Banks Peninsula*
- Timaru
- Oamaru
- **OTAGO**
- Moeraki
- **SOUTHLAND**
- **DUNEDIN**
- Riverton
- **INVERCARGILL**
- Bluff

STEWART ISLAND/RAKIURA

Northland

With warm, humid summers and mild winters, this region truly deserves its nickname 'The Winterless North'. About 250 km long and just 80 km across at its widest point, Northland tapers to the narrow northernmost tip of New Zealand, Cape Reinga, where the Pacific Ocean and Tasman Sea collide.

Steeped in Maori and pioneer history, Northland is the least urbanised region of New Zealand. This is a mystical, laid-back place where people know how to make their own fun. When they're not at sea they're on the golf course, horse riding, or sand tobogganing. Locals fish with friends and family or share their secret spots with tourists who flock here to experience surf-cast, deep water and game fishing.

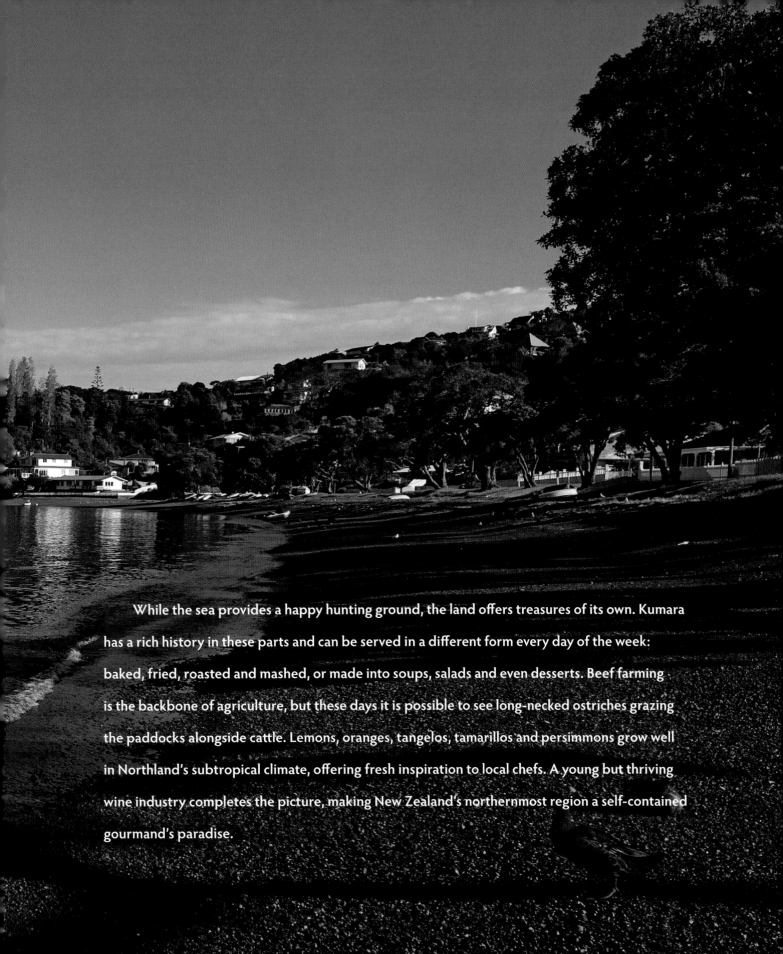

While the sea provides a happy hunting ground, the land offers treasures of its own. Kumara has a rich history in these parts and can be served in a different form every day of the week: baked, fried, roasted and mashed, or made into soups, salads and even desserts. Beef farming is the backbone of agriculture, but these days it is possible to see long-necked ostriches grazing the paddocks alongside cattle. Lemons, oranges, tangelos, tamarillos and persimmons grow well in Northland's subtropical climate, offering fresh inspiration to local chefs. A young but thriving wine industry completes the picture, making New Zealand's northernmost region a self-contained gourmand's paradise.

The tranquil waterfront at Russell in the Bay of Islands is backed by The Strand, a street of historic homes.

Manuka-smoked eel, apple *ajo blanco*, *migas* and avocado sorbet

SERVES 4 AS AN ENTRÉE

Ajo blanco

about 4 slices stale, good-quality bread,
    crusts removed
500 ml cold water
180 g ground almonds
2 Granny Smith apples, peeled and cored
2 cloves garlic, peeled
2 tablespoons sherry vinegar
6 tablespoons extra virgin olive oil
salt and freshly ground black pepper

Migas

200 g stale, good-quality bread
1 clove garlic, peeled and crushed
3 tablespoons extra virgin olive oil
salt
½ teaspoon sweet smoked Spanish paprika

Avocado sorbet

200 g sugar
2 tablespoons glucose syrup
400 ml water
3 avocados, peeled and stoned
juice of 2 limes
1 tablespoon inverted sugar

Smoked eel

150 g manuka-smoked eel, skinned (or use
    smoked snapper or hapuku)
1 Granny Smith apple
1 teaspoon poppy seeds

To make the *ajo blanco*, soak the bread in the water for 5 minutes, then place in a blender along with the almonds, apple, garlic and vinegar and purée until very smooth. With the machine still running, slowly add the olive oil. Season to taste with salt, pepper and extra vinegar if necessary. Pass through a sieve, then transfer to a serving jug and place in the refrigerator to chill for at least 1 hour.

To make the *migas*, place the bread and garlic in a food processor and process until rough breadcrumbs form.

   Heat the olive oil in a wide frying pan over a medium heat. Fry the breadcrumbs until golden brown, stirring often. Season to taste with salt and smoked paprika.

To make the avocado sorbet, place the sugar, syrup and water into a saucepan and heat until the sugar and glucose dissolve. Leave to cool to room temperature.

   Place the avocados into a food processor with the lime juice and process until smooth. With the machine still running slowly pour in the glucose, sugar and water solution, then finally the inverted sugar. Freeze the sorbet in an ice-cream machine according to the manufacturer's instructions.

To serve, slice the eel into .5 cm thick strips and divide between 4 bowls, placing it to the side. Slice the apple into matchstick-sized pieces, mix with the poppy seeds and place opposite the eel in the bowls. Place some *migas* in each bowl and top with the avocado sorbet. Serve and pour the *ajo blanco* at the table.

Carrington Resort – A Heritage Hotel, Maitai Bay, Karikari Peninsula

Northland features an indented coastline of bays and harbours, quiet coves, rocky shores and numerous sandy beaches.

Dijon lamb rack with smoked bacon jus and dauphine potatoes

SERVES 4 AS A MAIN COURSE

Dauphine potatoes

2 kg Agria potatoes, peeled and chopped
250 ml milk
100 g butter
125 g plain flour
3 eggs
oil for deep frying

Smoked bacon jus

2–3 rashers smoked bacon
about ½ cup red wine
about ½ cup beef stock
salt and pepper

4 baby lamb racks (allow a 4–6 rib rack
    per person)
oil for frying
2 courgettes (zucchini), sliced
Dijon mustard

To make the dauphine potatoes, cook the potatoes in boiling, salted water until tender. Drain well and mash thoroughly, preferably in a ricer.

Place the milk and butter into a saucepan and bring to the boil. Remove from the heat and stir in the flour, mixing well with a wooden spoon.

Add the eggs one at a time, beating well after each addition. Stir this mixture through the mashed potatoes, then pipe into desired shapes. Deep fry until golden brown.

To make the smoked bacon jus, cut the bacon into fine strips. Sauté in a frying pan for 1–2 minutes, then cover with red wine and simmer to reduce to one-quarter. Add the beef stock or glaze and further reduce until thick. Season to taste.

Preheat the oven to 180°C.

Season the lamb racks and heat a little oil in a heavy-based frying pan. Sear the lamb on each side, then transfer to an ovenproof dish and roast for about 15 minutes or until cooked to your liking.

Steam the courgettes until just tender.

To serve, spread the mustard over the lamb racks. Arrange on plates with dauphine potatoes and courgettes, and spoon over the smoked bacon jus.

Kamakura, Russell, Bay of Islands

Manuka honey and poppy seed parfait with sparkling raspberry jelly

SERVES 4–6

Poppy seed parfait
600 ml cream
6 egg yolks
180 g sugar
80 g manuka honey
100 ml white wine
40 g poppy seeds

Raspberry jellies
250 g fresh raspberries
4 sheets gelatine
125 ml water
100 g sugar
200 ml sparkling wine or champagne

Raspberry coulis
75 g icing sugar
fresh berries or fresh peppermint leaves
    to garnish

To make the parfait, whip the cream until stiff peaks form.

Place the egg yolks, sugar, honey and wine into a separate metal bowl and whisk continuously over a medium heat, until the mixture becomes thick and frothy. Take care not to let the mixture become too hot, and remove from the heat if necessary while whisking. This mixture is called a sabayon.

Once it is thick, pour the sabayon into a food processor and process until it has cooled. Carefully fold in the whipped cream and poppy seeds.

Spoon the mixture into pudding moulds, and freeze until solid.

To make the raspberry jellies, place 2–3 raspberries into each compartment of an ice cube tray.

Soak the gelatine in cold water until soft and malleable. Remove from the water.

Place the water and sugar into a saucepan and stir over a medium heat until warm and the sugar is completely dissolved. Remove from heat.

Mix together the gelatine, sugar syrup and sparkling wine. Pour over the raspberries and place in the refrigerator to set.

To make the raspberry coulis, place the remaining raspberries and the icing sugar into a food processor and process until liquidised. Strain to remove seeds.

To serve, remove the parfaits from their moulds and arrange on plates with several jellies. Drizzle over the coulis and garnish with fresh berries or peppermint leaves.

Kamakura, Russell, Bay of Islands

Russell in the Bay of Islands was New Zealand's first European settlement, first capital and is its oldest town.

Hapuku on mushroom tagliatelle

SERVES 2 AS A MAIN COURSE

Pasta

200 g flour
2 eggs
1 teaspoon extra virgin olive oil
pinch of paprika
pinch of salt

Mushroom sauce

20 g butter
1 small onion, peeled and chopped
2 cloves garlic
40 g mushrooms, sliced
2 rashers bacon, finely chopped
50 ml white wine
150 ml cream
100 ml chicken stock
20 ml jus

Vegetables

100 g beans, trimmed
6 asparagus spears, trimmed
other seasonal vegetables of your
    choice, e.g. carrots, coloured peppers
    (capsicums), courgettes (zucchini),
    broccoli, all finely julienned or sliced
a little butter for frying
2 tablespoons diced onion

Hapuku

2 hapuku fillets, skinned and boned
pinch of lime kelp
pinch of lemon pepper
pinch of flaked sea salt
olive oil for frying
a little butter
juice of 1 lemon
1 teaspoon truffle oil

To make the pasta, mix the flour, eggs, olive oil, paprika and salt together to form a firm ball, wrap in plastic food wrap and place in the refrigerator overnight.

The next day use a pasta machine to make the tagliatelle, or roll the dough out on a well-floured surface and cut into strips.

Bring a large saucepan of salted water to the boil and add the pasta.

Cook until al dente, then cool under cold running water.

To make the mushroom sauce, heat the butter in a frying pan and sauté the onion, garlic, mushrooms and bacon until golden.

Stir in the wine and let it bubble, then add the cream, stock and jus and reduce until creamy and thick.

Add the pasta and toss together well.

To prepare the vegetables, blanch the beans and asparagus and other vegetables of your choice for 2 minutes only.

Refresh immediately in iced water.

To serve, sauté the vegetables and onion in a little butter.

To prepare the hapuku, season the fish with lime kelp, lemon pepper and sea salt.

Preheat the oven to 140°C.

Heat a little olive oil in a frying pan and add the hapuku.

As the fish begins to turn white underneath, add some butter to the pan and turn the fish over.

Once seared on both sides transfer to an ovenproof dish and bake until cooked to your liking, about 4 minutes.

Alternatively, once the fish is seared, cover the pan but take it off the heat immediately.

Squeeze over the lemon juice and truffle oil and serve immediately on top of the hot pasta with mushroom sauce, with a side of vegetables.

Gannets International Feeding Ground, Russell, Bay of Islands

With many of the original European buildings on the seafront still standing, Russell's shops and restaurants create an atmosphere that reflects its settler history.

Kumara and smoked eel fritters with pumpkin, mushroom and haloumi salad and wasabi cream dressing

SERVES 4 AS AN ENTRÉE

Kumara and smoked eel fritters
350 g red kumara
4 spring onions, finely sliced
1 egg
100 g plain flour
1 tablespoon chopped coriander
250 g smoked eel
salt and pepper
olive oil for frying
2 lemons, halved to garnish

Pumpkin salad
250 g pumpkin, peeled and finely
    chopped
80 g button mushrooms, sliced
20 g pumpkin seeds
100 g mesclun
1 small red onion, peeled and finely sliced
80 g haloumi cheese
juice of 1 lemon
a little pumpkin seed oil

Wasabi cream dressing
1 teaspoon wasabi
200 ml crème fraîche
juice of ½ lemon
salt and pepper

To make the fritters, boil the unpeeled kumara whole.

Once they are cool enough to handle, peel and mash the kumara into a large bowl. Add the spring onions, egg, flour and coriander and mix until just combined.

Flake the smoked eel and gently fold through the kumara mixture, then season to taste.

Heat a little olive oil in a heavy-based frying pan over a medium heat. Place the lemons flesh-side down into the pan and sear until golden brown. Set aside.

Using the same frying pan, heat some more olive oil, and drop dessertspoonfuls of the fritter mixture into the oil. Cook the fritters until lightly browned, about 3 minutes. Turn the fritters and push down gently to ensure an even thickness. Cook on the other side until lightly browned and cooked through. Set aside and keep warm.

To make the pumpkin salad, preheat the oven to 200°C.

Place the pumpkin onto a baking tray or into a roasting dish and drizzle with a little olive oil. Roast for about 10 minutes, then add the mushrooms, pumpkin seeds and a little extra oil if necessary and roast for a further 8 minutes or until the pumpkin and mushrooms are cooked.

Place the mesclun, red onion and haloumi into a bowl. Add the roasted pumpkin and mushrooms, then squeeze over the lemon juice and a splash of pumpkin seed oil and gently toss together.

To make the wasabi cream dressing, whisk together the wasabi, crème fraîche and lemon juice in a small bowl and season to taste.

To serve, arrange 3 fritters in the centre of each plate with the pumpkin salad alongside. Spoon the wasabi dressing between the fritters and the salad and garnish with the seared lemon halves.

Waikokopu Café, Waitangi, Bay of Islands

Black rice-crusted ostrich with watermelon salad

SERVES 4 AS A MAIN COURSE

Watermelon dressing

700 g fresh watermelon, roughly chopped
⅛ teaspoon tartaric acid
2 tablespoons lemon juice
2 tablespoons orange juice
1 clove garlic, peeled and crushed
1 teaspoon sumac
¼ teaspoon cumin seeds
1 teaspoon raw sugar
4 fresh curry leaves
pinch of tandoori curry powder
3 tablespoons peach vinegar
½ teaspoon Dijon mustard
250 ml olive oil
sea salt and freshly ground mixed pepper

Salad

400 g ostrich back fillet
10 tablespoons black rice powder
4 tablespoons peanut oil
200 g fresh watermelon, diced
140 g good-quality feta
50 g quinoa, par boiled
30 g flaked almonds, lightly toasted
30 g pea shoots or baby sunflower shoots
30 g sango (radish) sprouts
15 g basil leaves
50 g currants, soaked in tea until plump

To make the watermelon dressing, place the watermelon into a food processor or blender and purée until liquid.

Place the watermelon juice, tartaric acid, lemon and orange juice into a saucepan and cook over a medium heat until thick and reduced by one-third.

Remove from the heat and strain into a stainless steel or glass bowl.

Add the garlic, sumac, cumin seeds (these are best soaked in cold water for 5 minutes then dried in the oven at 180°C until fragrant), sugar, curry leaves and powder, vinegar and mustard. Lastly whisk in the olive oil to make a vinaigrette. Set aside for at least 30–60 minutes before straining again.

Preheat the oven to 220°C.

Coat the ostrich meat thoroughly in the black rice powder.

Place the peanut oil in a heavy-based frying pan and heat until very hot. Sear the ostrich all over, then transfer to an ovenproof dish and roast for 1–3 minutes. Set aside to rest.

Place the watermelon in a bowl and crumble over the feta. Toss through the quinoa, almonds, pea shoots, sango sprouts, basil leaves and currants.

Dress lightly with the watermelon dressing and toss together.

To serve, slice the ostrich thinly across the grain and arrange over the salad.

Pure Tastes, Paihia, Bay of Islands

The many waterways of the Bay of Islands are fringed with pohutukawa trees, ablaze in crimson blossom in early summer.

Crayfish and fennel ravioli with saffron citrus butter

SERVES 4–5 AS AN ENTRÉE

Crayfish and fennel ravioli

1 fennel bulb, finely sliced

oil for frying

1 uncooked crayfish (or use a firm white-
    fleshed fish such as snapper or gurnard,
    or even scallops, if you prefer)

rock or sea salt

400 g packet fresh lasagne sheets
    (or 40 wonton wrappers)

1 egg, lightly beaten

Saffron citrus butter

150 g butter

generous pinch of saffron

zest of 1 lemon

zest of 1 orange

zest of 1 lime

fresh flat-leaf parsley for garnishing

To make the ravioli, place the fennel into a saucepan with a little oil and sauté gently until quite mushy.

Remove the meat from the crayfish. Place into a food processor along with the cooked fennel and process until well minced. Season to taste.

If using pasta sheets, roll them out until they are very thin, almost transparent.

Cut pasta sheets into 200 x 100 mm rectangles. Place a generous tablespoonful of crayfish mixture at one end of the rectangle. Brush around the mixture with beaten egg, then fold in half. Cut into a large round. Repeat this process until you have used up all the crayfish and fennel mixture.

To make the saffron citrus butter, melt the butter over a low heat along with the saffron and citrus zest. Simmer for at least 30 minutes, taking care not to burn it.

Bring a large saucepan of salted water to the boil, then cook the ravioli for about 3–4 minutes or until just cooked.

To serve, arrange the ravioli on plates with a generous serving of saffron butter and garnish with parsley.

Copthorne Hotel & Resort Hokianga, Omapere

An old jetty on the Hokianga, a quiet harbour on Northland's west coast with just a few sleepy settlements on its shores.

Looking north from Arai te Uru, the south head of Hokianga Harbour, to the huge dramatic sand dunes on the north head, piled up by westerly winds.

Auckland & the Hauraki Gulf

Most cities would be content with one harbour. Lucky Auckland boasts two. The Manukau provides safe haven from the rugged west coast while the sparkling Waitemata offers a playground between the central city and Auckland's north shore. To the northeast, the Hauraki Gulf wraps itself around myriad islands great and small.

Whatever the weather, Aucklanders are drawn to the coast. Youngsters learn to sail and kite surfers soar in the east coast breeze while long-boarders seek the perfect wave out west. Fishing from wharves, rocks or boats is another enduring pastime. Fortunate fishers might have something for the frying pan that evening. Otherwise, they can head to a local restaurant and enjoy Fish of the Day hooked by somebody else.

The gifts of the ocean are matched by gorgeous fruit and vegetables harvested from rich volcanic soil. Come summer, locally grown peppers and tomatoes work their sweet magic on menus around town. Cooler weather brings root vegetables from Auckland's southern outskirts to chefs' benches, while produce grown in giant glasshouses offers a year-round supply of culinary options.

On the site of some of New Zealand's original grape-growing areas, vineyard restaurants in Auckland's northwest display their own gastronomic flair matched with some outstanding wines.

Over on Waiheke Island, a flourishing wine and food culture means visitors and locals can enjoy a fabulous meal, glass of wine or cup of top-notch coffee any day of the week. East coast, west coast, city or island, in this part of the country you're totally spoiled for choice.

St Heliers Beach looks out to the pohutukawa-covered slopes of Rangitoto Island. A scenic waterfront drive from downtown Auckland takes in the popular eastern city beaches of Orakei, Mission Bay, Kohimarama and St Heliers.

Seared salmon fillet with Turkish coleslaw

SERVES 4 AS A MAIN COURSE

Turkish coleslaw

¼ red cabbage, finely sliced

½ red onion, peeled and finely sliced

1 medium carrot, peeled and cut into
matchsticks

1 tablespoon salt

2 Lebanese cucumbers, halved lengthways
and deseeded

2 cups fresh flat-leaf parsley

juice of 3 lemons

olive oil

Salmon

4 x 180 g salmon fillets, skin on

salt and pepper

olive oil for frying

hollandaise sauce, citrus mayonnaise or
crème fraîche for serving (optional)

To make the coleslaw, mix together the red cabbage, red onion and carrot in a medium-sized bowl. Stir through the salt and leave in the refrigerator for at least 3 hours.

Slice the cucumber finely and add to the cabbage along with the parsley. Add the lemon juice and a little olive oil. The salad should taste a little salty and sour. Set aside for 15 minutes.

Preheat the oven to 220°C.

To prepare the salmon, heat a little olive oil in a heavy-based frying pan. Season the fillets with salt and pepper and fry skin-side down for 2 minutes, making sure the skin doesn't burn. Turn the fillets over and cook in the oven for a further 4 minutes or until medium.

To serve, arrange the coleslaw in the centre of 4 serving plates and pour over a little pink liquid from the coleslaw. Place the salmon skin-side up on the coleslaw.

If you wish, serve with hollandaise sauce, citrus mayonnaise or crème fraîche.

Long Bay Restaurant, Long Bay, Auckland

Rangitoto Island seen from Narrow Neck Beach. Auckland's North Shore City boasts numerous fine beaches looking out to the harbour and gulf.

Sautéed prawns with chilli popcorn and sour cream

SERVES 4 AS AN ENTRÉE

400 g prawns, peeled and deveined
2 cloves garlic, peeled and chopped
1 fresh chilli, deseeded and chopped
4 tablespoons olive oil
1 fresh chilli, deseeded and halved
30 g popcorn kernels
juice of ½ lemon
3 tablespoons chopped fresh flat-leaf
    parsley
salt and pepper
150 ml sour cream
chilli powder for serving

Halve the prawns lengthways, and place in a bowl with the garlic and the first chilli. Set aside to marinate.

Heat 2 tablespoons of the oil in a medium-sized lidded frying pan. Heat until the oil is almost smoking, then throw in the chilli halves and popcorn and cover. Once the popping noise is at a high level, turn the heat right down to finish cooking the popcorn without burning it. Lift the lid carefully to check if the popcorn is ready, then using a slotted spoon remove from the oil and set aside to drain on paper towels.

Mix together the lemon juice, parsley, salt and pepper and sour cream and spoon onto a serving dish.

Heat the remaining 2 tablespoons of oil in a frying pan and quickly sauté the prawns until they are golden and just cooked.

Arrange the prawns on the sour cream dressing

Dust a little chilli powder and salt over the popcorn, then sprinkle the popcorn on top of the prawns. Serve immediately.

Soul Bar and Bistro, Viaduct Harbour, Auckland

Auckland's Viaduct Basin on the waterfront is where the America's Cup yacht syndicates have been based during Cup challenges and defences.

Roasted double snapper fillet with harissa, Israeli couscous and vincotto

SERVES 6 AS A MAIN COURSE

Harissa

3 red peppers (capsicums)

a little olive oil

juice of ½ lemon

½ teaspoon ground coriander

½ teaspoon ground cumin

½ teaspoon crushed garlic

few drops of Tabasco sauce

25 ml extra virgin olive oil

salt and pepper

Israeli couscous

about 400 ml chicken stock

oil for frying

½ red onion, peeled and finely chopped

1 teaspoon crushed garlic

300 g Israeli couscous

150 g semi-dried tomatoes in oil, chopped

bunch of fresh coriander, chopped

zest of 1 lemon

30 ml extra virgin olive oil

Snapper

6 x 700 g whole snapper, scales removed, skin on

salt and pepper

olive oil for frying

cabernet vincotto for drizzling

extra virgin olive oil for drizzling

To make the harissa, preheat the oven to 180°C.

Rub the peppers in a little olive oil and roast in the oven until they blister. Set aside to cool. Once they are cool enough to handle, rub off the skins and remove the seeds.

Place the peppers, lemon juice, coriander, cumin, and garlic into a food processor or blender and purée until smooth. With the food processor still running, add the Tabasco, extra virgin olive oil and season to taste.

To prepare the couscous, place the stock into a saucepan and heat gently.

Heat a little olive oil in a frying pan and gently sauté the onion and garlic until softened. Stir in the couscous and fry for 3 minutes. Add enough hot stock to just cover the couscous and simmer until tender, about 7–8 minutes. Remove from the heat and set aside to cool.

Stir through the chopped tomatoes, coriander and lemon peel along with the extra virgin olive oil.

To prepare the snapper, fillet the fish from the head down to the tail but leave the tail attached on both sides. Cut out the backbone, leaving the two fillets joined at the tail. Carefully remove fine bones from fillets.

Preheat the oven to 180°C.

Season the fish and smear the inside with harissa.

Heat a heavy-based frying pan and quickly sear the fish on both sides in a little olive oil, then transfer to a baking tray.

Roast for about 6 minutes.

Meanwhile, warm the couscous and divide between 6 plates. Arrange the fish on the couscous and drizzle with vincotto and extra virgin olive oil.

Harbourside, Auckland Central

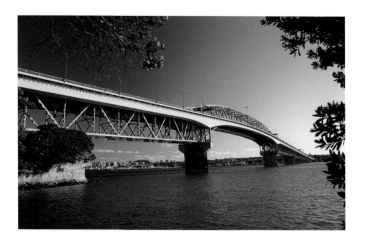

Auckland Harbour Bridge (above), linking Auckland city and the North Shore, and the high-rise panorama of Auckland city (right), dominated by the 328-metre Sky Tower.

Chocolate cake

200 g dark chocolate chunks

50 g Valrhona chocolate

200 g caster sugar

160 g unsalted butter

40 ml water

4 eggs, whisked

40 ml brandy

Hazelnut praline wafer

200 g sugar

50 g hazelnuts, peeled

water

Cherry sauce

300 g caster sugar

150 ml juice from the cherries

500 g jar sour morello cherries, drained,
    but retain the juice

about ½ cup mascarpone for serving

white chocolate shavings for serving

a few extra sour morello cherries
    for serving

Chocolate truffle cakes with sweet and sour cherry sauce

MAKES 8 SMALL CAKES

To make the chocolate cake, preheat the oven to 90°C.

Place the chocolate in a bowl and melt gently over a saucepan of simmering water.

Place the sugar, butter and water into a separate saucepan and heat gently until the butter is melted. Stir the butter mixture into the melted chocolate. Stir in the eggs and brandy.

Pour into 8 greased pudding moulds and bake for 25–35 minutes until set.

Once cooled, chill in the refrigerator until ready to serve.

Place the sugar into a saucepan and add enough cold water to come 1 cm above the sugar. Place over a gentle heat and stir until the sugar is dissolved. Simmer until the mixture turns golden in colour, then add the chopped hazelnuts and stir to coat. Turn out onto a sheet of baking paper to cool for at least 30 minutes.

Preheat the oven to 150°C.

Crush the coated nuts with a rolling pin, then transfer to a food processor and pulse to a coarse powder.

Spread the powdered nuts over a clean sheet of baking powder and bake for about 5 minutes until the sugar has melted. Remove from the oven and set aside to cool.

Snap off shards to serve.

To make the cherry sauce, place the sugar in a saucepan and heat very slowly, stirring gently and continuously, until it starts to caramelise.

Stir in the cherry juice, then add the cherries and bring to the boil.

Place the sauce into a blender and purée until smooth, then pass through a fine sieve.

To serve, slide the chilled cakes out of their moulds and place in serving bowls. Carefully pour a little cherry sauce around each cake and top with mascarpone. Garnish with white chocolate shavings, a few preserved cherries, and a shard of hazelnut praline wafer.

Hammerheads Restaurant, Okahu Bay, Auckland

Cured salmon with shaved fennel, baby capers and verjuice dressing

SERVES 5–6 AS AN ENTRÉE

Cured salmon

200 g salt

200 g caster sugar

¼ vanilla pod, split, seeds scraped and finely chopped

1 tablespoon crushed black peppercorns

1 side salmon, skin on, fine bones removed

100 ml lemon oil

2 tablespoons chopped fresh coriander

½ lemon, thinly sliced

3½ tablespoons brandy

Verjuice dressing

500 ml Riesling verjuice

¼ vanilla pod, split and seeds scraped out and reserved

3½ tablespoons extra virgin olive oil

juice of ¼ lemon

For serving

½ bulb fennel, very thinly sliced for serving

½ cup baby capers for serving

olive oil for drizzling

micro salad greens for garnishing

To make the cured salmon, mix together the salt, sugar, chopped vanilla pod and seeds and peppercorns.

Cut the salmon in half lengthways, brush both halves of the salmon with lemon oil and sprinkle the coriander over. Place 1 half skin-side down on a large piece of plastic food wrap.

Cover the salmon with the salt and sugar mixture, arrange lemon slices on top and sprinkle with brandy and a little more salt and sugar mixture. Carefully lay the second salmon half on top, skin-side up, and wrap both together in the plastic food wrap.

Leave the salmon to cure for 2 days in the refrigerator.

To make the verjuice dressing, place the verjuice and vanilla pod and seeds in a saucepan over a medium heat. Bring gently to the boil, and reduce by half. Take off the heat and remove the vanilla pod. Once cooled, whisk in the oil and lemon juice.

Once the salmon has cured, gently wipe off any excess salt and sugar with absorbent kitchen paper.

Slice the salmon thinly and arrange on flat plates. Sprinkle over fennel, capers and verjuice dressing. Drizzle over a little olive oil and garnish with a few micro salad leaves.

Hammerheads Restaurant, Okahu Bay, Auckland

Waikanae crab lasagne with lemon butter sauce

SERVES 8–10 AS AN ENTRÉE OR LIGHT LUNCH

Béchamel sauce
50 g butter
50 g plain flour
500 ml milk

Filling
50 g butter
½ cup diced onion
500 g Waikanae crabmeat
50 g freshly grated Parmesan cheese
about 1 cup chopped fresh parsley
salt and pepper
cayenne pepper
2 leeks, well washed and finely sliced
1 tablespoon butter
250 g ricotta cheese

Lasagne
4 sheets fresh lasagne (or use pre-cooked
    dry lasagne sheets)
butter
freshly grated Parmesan cheese for
    sprinkling

Lemon butter sauce
juice of 2 lemons
200 g cold butter, diced
salt and pepper

fresh micro greens for garnishing

Preheat the oven to 160°C.

To make the béchamel sauce, melt the butter in a saucepan, stir in the flour and cook for 1–2 minutes. Gradually add the milk, a little at a time, stirring continuously. Stir until the sauce is thickened and smooth.

To make the filling, melt the butter in a heavy-based saucepan. Add the onion and sauté until softened but not brown. Add the crabmeat and sauté for 5 minutes, then stir in the béchamel sauce, Parmesan and parsley. Season to taste with the salt, pepper and cayenne – you should be able to taste just a hint of cayenne. Set aside to cool.

In another heavy-based saucepan, sauté the leeks in the butter until just softened, then stir in the ricotta and season to taste.

To assemble the lasagne, butter a gratin dish or roasting pan, about 30 cm x 20 cm.

Line the dish with a sheet of pasta cut to fit. Spread over one-third of the leek and ricotta mixture, then one third of the crab filling and top with another pasta sheet.

Repeat with the remaining mixtures, then dot the top sheet of pasta with a little butter and sprinkle the Parmesan over.

Cover the dish with aluminium foil and bake for 40 minutes. Leave to cool slightly for about 10–15 minutes, then cut into squares.

To make the lemon butter sauce, place the lemon juice in a small saucepan and bring to the boil over a medium–high heat. As soon as the juice is boiling, add the butter and whisk over the heat until the butter is melted and the sauce is smooth. Season to taste.

Serve slices of lasagne with lemon butter sauce and garnished with micro greens.

Mikano, Mechanics Bay, Auckland

The Viaduct Basin (above) and nearby Mechanics Bay are home to myriad watercraft of all descriptions, including fishing boats, container ships, superyachts and racing craft.

Wild venison loin with slow-roasted beets and sauce soubise

SERVES 6 AS A MAIN COURSE

Sauce soubise

1 brown onion, peeled and finely chopped
1 clove garlic, peeled and chopped
100 g unsalted butter
3½ tablespoons white wine
100 ml cream

Slow-roasted beets

600 g baby beetroot, washed
¼ cup balsamic vinegar
⅛ cup red wine vinegar
½ teaspoon flaky sea salt
½ teaspoon freshly ground black pepper
¼ cup extra virgin olive oil
1 teaspoon fresh oregano
1 teaspoon fresh tarragon
extra virgin olive oil for serving

Venison

about 950 g–1 kg venison shortloin
salt and pepper
2 tablespoons olive oil
300 g white asparagus spears
about 60 g venison salami, thinly sliced
olive oil for frying
6 artichoke hearts, halved
120 g macadamia nuts, toasted
about ½ cup fresh micro mustard greens
    for garnishing

To make the sauce soubise, place the onion, garlic and butter into a saucepan and sauté slowly over a low heat until just softened. Deglaze the pan with the wine and reduce by half. Add the cream and simmer for 2 minutes.

Place the sauce into a blender and purée until smooth, then pass through a fine sieve and set aside.

To prepare the beets, preheat the oven to 160°C.

Toss the beetroot, vinegars, salt, pepper, olive oil, oregano and tarragon together and place in a large roasting dish. Cover with aluminium foil and roast for about 1 hour.

When the beetroot are cool enough to handle, peel off the skin and discard. Toss in a little olive oil and set aside.

To prepare the venison, preheat the oven to 120°C.

Season the venison.

Heat the oil in a frying pan until very hot, then quickly brown the meat on all sides.

Transfer to an ovenproof dish and roast until rare, about 15 minutes. Let rest for 10 minutes before slicing.

Bring a large saucepan of salted water to the boil, blanch the asparagus, then refresh. Wrap the asparagus spears in the thinly sliced salami, then pan fry in a little oil.

To serve, spoon the sauce soubise onto plates and arrange the beetroot, artichokes and sliced venison on top. Serve the wrapped asparagus alongside and scatter over the macadamia nuts. Garnish with the micro mustard greens.

Mudbrick Vine Yard Restaurant, Waiheke Island

Pohutukawa, New Zealand's 'Christmas tree', grows naturally along the coastlines and in the coastal forests of the upper North Island and the islands of the Hauraki Gulf.

Grilled scampi with caponata and tomato pesto

SERVES 4–6 AS AN ENTRÉE

Dressing

2 tablespoons honey

150 ml white wine

150 ml white wine vinegar

3½ tablespoons olive oil

salt and pepper

Caponata

2 shallots, finely diced

4 tablespoons olive oil

2 Roma tomatoes, finely diced

1½ tablespoons red wine vinegar

salt and pepper

1 small eggplant (aubergine), finely diced

2 sticks celery, finely diced

1 red pepper (capsicum), deseeded, finely diced

1 yellow pepper (capsicum), deseeded, finely diced

1 courgette (zucchini), finely diced

1 clove garlic, peeled and crushed

50 g capers

50 g pine nuts, toasted

Tomato pesto

20 g pine nuts

50 g sundried tomatoes

1 teaspoon tomato purée

20 g freshly grated Parmesan cheese

2 tablespoons chopped fresh basil

100 ml extra virgin olive oil

salt and pepper

Scampi

12–18 New Zealand scampi, washed and halved from head to tail

salt and pepper

olive oil for frying

lemon wedges for garnishing

fresh basil or coriander leaves for garnishing

To make the dressing, place the honey, wine, vinegar and oil in a small saucepan, season to taste and cook over a low heat until syrupy. Set aside to cool.

To make the caponata, fry the shallots in 1 tablespoon of olive oil, then stir in the tomato, vinegar, salt and pepper. Cook briefly, then place in a medium-sized bowl.

Place the eggplant and 2 tablespoons of olive oil in the same frying pan and cook gently until golden brown, then stir into the tomato mixture.

In a frying pan sauté the celery, peppers, courgette and garlic with the remaining oil until just cooked, then season to taste.

Stir the vegetables into the tomato mixture and add the capers and pine nuts.

Toss through the prepared dressing and adjust seasoning if necessary.

To make the pesto, place the pine nuts, sundried tomatoes, tomato purée, Parmesan and basil into a food processor. Process roughly, then slowly add the olive oil until it forms a smooth paste, season to taste and set aside.

To prepare the scampi, heat a large frying pan or a barbecue hotplate. Season the scampi, brush with olive oil and pan fry or grill for about 1–2 minutes until just cooked.

To serve, spoon the caponata onto plates and arrange the scampi on top. Drizzle with tomato pesto and garnish with lemon wedges and fresh herbs.

Te Whau Vineyard and Restaurant, Waiheke Island

Coromandel, Bay of Plenty & Taranaki

Whether you're on a gleaming white sand beach in the Coromandel Peninsula or a glistening black sand beach in Taranaki, the sea tends to dictate the mood in this part of the country.

The Coromandel has over 400 kilometres of its own dazzling shoreline, stretching from the sheltered Firth of Thames on the west, north to Colville Channel and east to the southern Pacific Ocean. Where gold and silver mining once ruled, locals now make a living in arts, crafts and tourism. Chefs can design dishes around a rich variety of local produce, from salty mussels to creamy macadamia nuts. The relaxed lifestyle allows people plenty of time off to swim, kayak and snorkel.

The Coromandel Peninsula features some of the North Island's most stunning scenery. Wind and tide have sculpted the soft sandstone at Cathedral Cove into low caverns and stacks such as Te Hoho Rock.

Further south, a 100-kilometre sweep of beach that starts at Mount Maunganui and ends at Whakatane offers numerous pursuits, from fishing and diving to sailing and surfing. The Bay of Plenty is aptly named: kiwifruit hang in vast numbers from vines, avocados festoon the trees and feijoas, tamarillos and passionfruit provide a taste of the subtropics. Out west, surrounding Mount Taranaki's near-perfect 2518-metre cone, emerald paddocks produce white gold: decadent cheeses, silky ice creams and other gourmet milk products to tempt any palate. Eating is a major pastime, rivalling rugby, surfing, gardening and gallery-going, and it isn't hard to collect mussels from the rocks or pull a fish from the sea.

After dinner, active folk can be found taking in the sunset from spectacular cliff-top walkways and planning the next day's adventure.

Macadamia crumbed scallop kebabs

SERVES 4 AS AN ENTRÉE

Macadamia Lemon Kelp Sprinkle
¼ cup ground macadamia nuts
4 tablespoons tapioca flour
2 tablespoons lemon pepper
1 tablespoon powdered sea kelp

24 scallops
macadamia oil for frying
100 ml beer or wine
fresh salad greens for serving

8 bamboo skewers

To make the macadamia lemon kelp sprinkle, combine the ground nuts, flour, lemon pepper and kelp in a mixing bowl. Set aside.

Drain the excess liquid from the scallops and thread 3 scallops onto each skewer.
　　Lightly sprinkle each scallop kebab with the macadamia lemon kelp sprinkle.
　　Heat a thin layer of macadamia oil in a frying pan and sear the scallops for 1–2 minutes each side.
　　Remove the kebabs from the pan and arrange on a serving dish.
　　Deglaze the pan with the beer or wine, and heat until the sauce begins to bubble on the surface.
　　Arrange 2 scallop kebabs per person on each serving plate, pour over the sauce and serve with fresh salad greens.
　　Serve immediately.

Cathedral Cove Macadamias, Hahei beach, Coromandel

Coromandel's intricate island-studded coastline and inviting beaches are typified by Hahei Beach on the east of the peninsula.

Pan-roasted pork fillet with dates and apricots and a lemon cream sauce

SERVES 4 AS A MAIN COURSE

Pork

4 pork fillets

½ cup dates, pitted and chopped

½ cup dried apricots, chopped

small bunch of flat-leaf parsley, finely chopped

200 g butter

Marinade

2 tablespoons paprika

2 tablespoons mild curry powder

3 garlic cloves, peeled and finely chopped

2 teaspoons dried mixed herbs

6 tablespoons olive oil

Lemon cream sauce

juice of ½ lemon

100 ml cream

salt and pepper

potato mash for serving

green salad for serving

To prepare the pork, split the fillets and butterfly them open.

Mix together the dried fruit and parsley, and arrange the mixture down the middle of each fillet. Roll up the fillets, and place seam-side down in a dish.

To make the marinade, mix together all the ingredients and pour over the pork fillets. Set aside to marinate, covered, in the refrigerator for at least 3 hours.

Preheat the oven to 180°C.

Remove the pork from the marinade, and place into a roasting dish along with the butter. Roast for about 12–15 minutes.

Once the meat is cooked, remove the fillets and set aside to rest.

To make the lemon cream sauce, place the roasting dish with the pan juices on the stove-top. Stir in the lemon juice and cream and season to taste. Heat, stirring continuously, until the sauce has reduced and is of a pouring consistency.

To serve, spoon enough sauce to cover half of each plate, slice the fillets on the diagonal and arrange on the sauce.

Serve with potato mash and a green salad.

Eggsentric Café, Flaxmill Bay, Coromandel

With a mild, warm climate and abundant sandy beaches, the Coromandel Peninsula (above, right and overleaf) is a holidaymaker's paradise.

Pan-seared herb-crusted hapuku with anchovy sauce

SERVES 4 AS A MAIN COURSE

Herb crust

125 g mixed fresh herbs (parsley, fennel, thyme, chervil, celery, etc.)
2 cloves garlic, peeled and crushed
zest of ½ lemon
½ teaspoon salt
¼ teaspoon freshly ground black pepper
100 g butter, melted
75 g fresh bread

Anchovy sauce

100 g anchovies
1 clove garlic, peeled and crushed
5 peppercorns
1 bay leaf
sprig of fresh thyme
75 ml chicken stock
juice of 1 lemon
½ tablespoon chopped flat-leaf parsley
100 ml extra virgin olive oil

Hapuku

olive oil for frying
butter for frying
4 hapuku fillets

steamed asparagus for serving
potato mash for serving

To make the herb crust, place the herbs, garlic and lemon zest into a food processor and process until smooth. Add the salt, pepper, butter and bread and process further until blended and smooth.

Spread the resulting paste onto a sheet of baking paper, place another sheet on top and roll smooth with a rolling pin until the layer is about 2 mm thick. Freeze until needed.

To make the anchovy sauce, place the anchovies, garlic, peppercorns, bay leaf, thyme and chicken stock into a saucepan. Bring gently to the boil and cook for 5 minutes, then push through a strainer.

Return the sauce to the pan and stir in the lemon juice, parsley and oil – the mixture should be the consistency of a vinaigrette. Keep warm over a low heat.

To prepare the hapuku, preheat the oven to 180°C.

Heat a little olive oil and a knob of butter in a heavy-based frying pan.

Sear each hapuku fillet on 1 side only. Turn the fillets over and remove from the heat.

Take the herb crust from the freezer and cut out 4 pieces the same size as the fillets. Place a piece of crust on top of the uncooked side of each piece of fish.

Place in an ovenproof dish and bake for about 5–10 minutes, until just cooked. The timing will depend on the thickness of the fish.

Place steamed asparagus on 4 serving plates and top with fillets of fish. Serve with potato mash and anchovy sauce alongside.

Salt, Whitianga, Coromandel

Mussel fritters with sweet chilli sauce

SERVES 4 AS AN ENTRÉE

1½ cups plain flour
1 teaspoon baking powder
pinch of salt
2 eggs
about 1 cup milk
½ onion, peeled and finely chopped
2 teaspoons capers
18 mussels, lightly steamed
butter for frying
sweet chilli sauce and lemon wedges
    for serving

Place the flour, baking powder and salt into a bowl. Stir in the eggs and enough milk to make a runny consistency. (If the batter is too thick the fritters will be doughy.) Stir in the onion and capers.

Chop each mussel into 2–3 chunky pieces and stir through the batter.

Heat the butter in a frying pan until hot, then add tablespoonfuls of the batter and fry until golden and cooked both sides.

Serve with sweet chilli sauce and lemon wedges.

Hot Waves Café, Hot Water Beach, Coromandel

The Coromandel Peninsula is rugged, mountainous and densely forested, but is also home to some of the country's most dramatic and beautiful coastal scenery.

Warm salad of bacon-wrapped roasted pumpkin and haloumi with toasted sesame and honey dressing

SERVES 4 AS AN ENTRÉE

Salad

8 x .5 cm-thick slices haloumi cheese

handful of fresh thyme

⅛ small pumpkin, cut into 8 x .5 cm-thick slices

8 rashers free-range streaky bacon

olive oil for drizzling

2 cups watercress

4 tablespoons sango (radish) sprouts

2 oranges, peeled and segmented

Dressing

1 tablespoon wine vinegar

½ tablespoon honey

1 tablespoon sesame seeds, toasted

Preheat the oven to 175°C.

Arrange a slice of haloumi and a couple of sprigs of thyme on each slice of pumpkin, then wrap in bacon.

Place on a baking tray and drizzle with olive oil.

Roast for about 25 minutes or until the pumpkin has softened.

To make the dressing, whisk together the vinegar, honey and sesame seeds and season to taste.

Place the watercress, sprouts and oranges into a bowl and toss through with a little dressing.

To serve, arrange some salad on each plate and top with 2 slices of bacon-wrapped pumpkin. Drizzle extra dressing on the top.

Slowfish Beachfront Café, Mount Maunganui, Bay of Plenty

The resort of Mount Maunganui (above and opposite) sits on the seaward side of Tauranga Harbour, the region's busiest port. It comes alive in summer, with all manner of water-based activities.

Kingfish tartare with quark, capers and caviar

SERVES 4 AS AN ENTRÉE

Dressing
80 ml extra virgin olive oil
zest and juice of 1 lime
1 clove garlic, peeled and finely chopped
1 chilli, deseeded and finely chopped
salt and pepper

Kingfish tartare
400 g kingfish fillet
100 g quark cheese
salt and freshly ground black pepper
20 g capers, chopped
20 g caviar
handful of baby watercress

To make the dressing, whisk together the olive oil, lime juice and zest, garlic and chilli. Season to taste.

Slice the kingfish thinly, season and arrange on plates. Drizzle over the dressing.

Season the quark to taste, and spoon over the kingfish, then sprinkle with capers, caviar and watercress.

The Sebel Trinity Wharf Tauranga, Bay of Plenty

Just a few kilometres from Opotiki, Waiotahi is one of many long, sweeping beaches in the eastern Bay of Plenty. Motuhora (Whale) Island off Whakatane appears in the distance.

Manuka honey crème brûlée with kiwifruit gelato and pistachio biscotti

SERVES 4

Crème brûlée

6 egg yolks

30 g caster sugar

500 ml cream

½ cinnamon stick

30 g manuka honey

30 g caster sugar

Gelato

250 ml milk

seeds from ½ vanilla pod

2 eggs

¾ cup caster sugar

2 golden kiwifruit, peeled

Biscotti

3 egg whites

pinch of cream of tartar

½ cup caster sugar

¾ cup plain flour

zest of 3 limes

¾ cup pistachio nuts

To make the brûlée, preheat the oven to 150°C. Beat the egg yolks and first measure of caster sugar together until thick and pale.

Place the cream and cinnamon stick into a saucepan and heat until almost boiling. Stir in the honey. Remove the cream from the heat and stir in the egg yolk and sugar mixture. Strain the mixture and divide evenly between 4 ramekins.

Place the ramekins into an ovenproof dish, then pour enough boiling water into the dish to come halfway up the sides of the ramekins. Bake for about 30 minutes or until just set. Chill in the refrigerator until ready to serve.

Just before serving, sprinkle with the second measure of sugar and cook under a preheated grill or use a mini culinary blowtorch until the sugar caramelises.

To make the gelato, place the milk into a saucepan and add the seeds from the vanilla pod. Bring gently to the boil, then remove from the heat.

Combine the eggs and sugar in a bowl, then stir in the warm milk.

Return the milk mixture to the saucepan and heat gently, taking care not to boil or the egg will curdle. Stir continuously until the mixture coats the back of a spoon, then strain and set aside to chill in the refrigerator.

Place the kiwifruit into a food processor or blender and purée until smooth. Fold the puréed kiwifruit into the cold custard and pour into an ice-cream container. Place into the freezer and beat the mixture every hour until it is set to incorporate air into the gelato. Remove from the freezer about 30 minutes before serving.

To make the biscotti, preheat the oven to 180°C.

Grease a loaf tin and line with baking paper.

Beat the egg whites and cream of tartar together until soft peaks form. Add the sugar and beat until thick. Fold in the flour, lime zest and pistachio nuts, then spread into the loaf tin.

Bake for 40–45 minutes, remove from the oven and allow to cool completely.

Once the loaf is cold, preheat the oven to 140°C.

Slice the loaf into 5 mm thick biscuits and arrange on a baking tray. Place in the oven and allow the biscuits to dry for 25 minutes, turning after 15 minutes. Set aside to cool. Store any leftover biscotti in an airtight container, and if they go soft, dry them out in the oven again.

To serve, place a crème brulee ramekin on a serving plate alongside a ball of gelato and a finger of biscotti.

The Sebel Trinity Wharf Tauranga, Bay of Plenty

Enjoying the surf at Mount Maunganui. From Tauranga west to Opotiki there are mostly sandy shores, interrupted by headlands and estuaries.

Aged eye fillet with smoked Portobello mushrooms, horseradish foam and red wine jus

SERVES 4 AS A MAIN COURSE

Potato hash cake
10 baby potatoes, peeled
1 tablespoon oil
1 onion, peeled and finely chopped
250 g pancetta, finely chopped
handful of finely chopped fresh thyme
    and rosemary

Red wine jus
250 ml red wine
2 litres beef stock
2 sprigs fresh rosemary

Smoked mushrooms
4 large Portobello mushrooms, peeled
olive oil for drizzling
salt and pepper

Eye fillet
800–900 g piece eye fillet
about 2 tablespoons oil for frying

Horseradish foam
300 ml cream
1 tablespoon horseradish
salt and pepper

fresh micro salad greens for garnishing

To make the potato hash cake, cook the potatoes in boiling salted water until tender. Drain and transfer to a large mixing bowl. Once the potatoes are cool enough to handle, crush them with your hands, or with a fork.

To prepare the red wine jus, place the wine into a saucepan and bring to the boil. Reduce until thick and syrupy, then add the beef stock and rosemary and simmer over a low heat for about 30 minutes until thickened.

Preheat the oven to 180°C.
    Heat the oil in a frying pan and gently sauté the onion and pancetta until the onion is softened. Stir the onion and pancetta through the crushed potato, along with the fresh herbs.
    Shape the potato mixture into 4 even-sized potato cakes and place on a baking tray. Bake for about 10 minutes until golden. The potato cakes can be prepared in advance and reheated when needed.

To prepare the mushrooms, place the mushrooms on a baking tray and drizzle with olive oil and season to taste.
    Bake at 180°C until the mushrooms are half cooked, then transfer to a smoking rack and smoke for 4 minutes. Alternatively, bake the mushrooms until cooked.

To make the horseradish foam, place the cream, horseradish and salt and pepper to taste into a saucepan and bring slowly to the boil. Simmer until it has reduced to a sauce-like consistency and will coat the back of a spoon.
    Foam using a stick blender.

To prepare the steak, trim the fillet and cut into 4 even-sized pieces. Heat the oil in a heavy-based frying pan and cook the meat on both sides until done to your liking. Rest before serving.

To serve, spoon some red wine jus onto each plate, arrange the steak then a mushroom on top, and drizzle over horseradish sauce. Serve with the potato cake and some fresh micro greens as a garnish.

Kestrel at the Landing, Tauranga, Bay of Plenty

Oven-baked snapper with lemon and garlic olive oil on wilted greens, baby potatoes and blistered cherry tomatoes

SERVES 4 AS A MAIN COURSE

Garlic olive oil

3 cloves garlic, peeled and crushed

6 tablespoons olive oil

Potatoes

800 g small new potatoes

50 g butter

1 yellow pepper (capsicum), deseeded and chopped

1 red pepper (capsicum), deseeded and chopped

small bunch of chopped flat-leaf parsley

Balsamic dressing

75 ml olive oil

1½ tablespoons balsamic vinegar

½ teaspoon Dijon mustard

Snapper

800 g snapper fillets (or other firm white fish)

salt and pepper

2 lemons, finely sliced

Vegetables

12 cherry tomatoes

12 kalamata olives

800 g bok choy, well washed

Combine the garlic with the first measure of olive oil and set aside to infuse.

Cook the potatoes in their skins in boiling, salted water, and drain when just cooked. Set aside to cool, then cut into quarters.

Gently stir the olive oil, balsamic vinegar and mustard together, taking care not to blend it too much.

Preheat the oven to 180°C.

Place the fish fillets in an ovenproof dish, then drizzle over 4 tablespoons of the garlic-infused olive oil. Lightly season and arrange the lemon slices on top of the fish. Set aside.

Melt the butter in an ovenproof frying pan, and stir in the potatoes, peppers, parsley and salt and pepper to taste. Place in the same ovenproof dish as the fish and place in the oven.

Bake for about 10 minutes until the fish is just cooked through.

Heat another frying pan with the remaining garlic oil in it, and toss the cherry tomatoes and olives, just long enough to blister the tomatoes and warm the olives.

Cook the bok choy in boiling, salted water for a few minutes until it just softens.

To serve, arrange the potatoes and capsicums in the centre of 4 large dinner plates, place the olives and tomatoes around the potatoes and drizzle over the balsamic dressing. Carefully arrange the bok choy on the potatoes, and top with the fish and slices of lemon. Serve immediately.

Okurukuru Winery, Taranaki

Along the North Taranaki coast near Tongaporutu the sea has fashioned unusual shapes from the sandstone.

Scallop and black tiger prawn linguine

SERVES 4 AS AN ENTRÉE

500 g dried linguine pasta

½ teaspoon olive oil

¼ cup extra virgin olive oil

400 g fresh New Zealand scallops

400 g black tiger prawns, peeled and deveined

2 medium-sized red onions, peeled and finely sliced

1 clove garlic, peeled and finely sliced

2 long fresh red chillies, deseeded and finely sliced

100 g kalamata olives, pitted

1 x 200 g jar or can artichoke hearts, drained and quartered

handful of chopped fresh flat leaf parsley

¼ cup freshly grated Parmesan cheese

juice of 2 lemons

salt and pepper

4 lemons, quartered for serving

chopped fresh tomatoes for serving (optional)

Parmesan croûtes

½ cup freshly grated Parmesan cheese

Bring a large saucepan of salted water to the boil and add the first measure of olive oil to prevent the pasta sticking together. Add the pasta and stir immediately to ensure the strands separate. Cook for 10 minutes, stirring twice, until the pasta is al dente. Drain and refresh under cold running water, then set aside to drain in a colander.

It is best to cook the remaining ingredients in 2 separate frying pans, as this ensures even, fast cooking of the seafood. If using only 1 frying pan, make sure it is large enough that the ingredients can be seared quickly without stewing, and the pasta can be comfortably tossed through.

Separate the ingredients into 2 batches. Heat the 2 frying pans until very hot, then add half the extra virgin olive oil to each pan.

Add the scallops, prawns and onions to each pan, and sear, using tongs to turn the scallops and prawns individually. Add the garlic, chillies, olives and artichokes and sauté for a further 5 minutes or until fragrant and the seafood is just cooked.

Add half the cooked pasta to each pan along with the parsley, Parmesan and lemon juice. Season to taste. Toss all the ingredients together well, and allow a minute or so for the pasta to reheat and the Parmesan to melt.

To make the Parmesan croûtes, bake small mounds of freshly grated Parmesan cheese at 180°C until golden. When these are removed from the oven the cheese will crisp as it cools. The croûtes can be made in advance if desired.

Serve in bowls with lemon wedges, chopped fresh tomatoes and Parmesan croûtes on the side.

Salt, The Waterfront Hotel, New Plymouth, Taranaki

At Tongaporutu are the landmark pillars of the Three Sisters. Storms have now largely eroded the smallest sister.

East Coast, Hawke's Bay & Wellington

Rounding the East Cape, through the Hawke's Bay to Wellington, you are never far from the ocean. East Coast locals are the first to see the sunrise, and farmers and fishers are often hard at work before first light.

Further south, Gisborne's primary producers are renowned for their meat products, sweetcorn, squash, tangy citrus and wine — especially delicious Chardonnay. When they're not working, they're playing: this is a top spot for surfing and fishing.

In Hawke's Bay, the fertile soils of the alluvial plains are refreshed by seasonal flooding, ensuring that vegetables and pip fruit remain abundant. Vineyards criss-cross the countryside, producing top-class wines with an international reputation.

Napier celebrates its world-famous art deco heritage with an annual festival. The rest of the year, locals spend their spare time at the races, on the golf course, at sea or in the sky, flying, gliding and parachuting.

Wellington, a city where houses cling to the hills and stunning views are a dime a dozen, has a flourishing arts, culture and entertainment scene. People flock to theatre, live music, galleries and museums or indulge in outdoor pursuits, such as sailing, mountain-biking and bushwalking. Nothing beats the beauty of Wellington Harbour on a blue-sky day. Fish abound in these cool, clear waters and feature daily on blackboard menus, prepared by skilled chefs. In a city known for its creativity, fresh food and original ideas combine to create something really special.

The cliffs of Te Mata Peak overlook the Tukituki River winding its way to the broad sweep of Hawke's Bay.

Bruschetta with stir-fried vegetables and sweet pickled walnut spread

SERVES 4 AS AN ENTRÉE

Bruschetta

1 loaf ciabatta bread

garlic oil or olive oil for drizzling

Vegetables

2 teaspoons cooking oil

½ teaspoon crushed garlic

1 cup chopped mixed seasonal vegetables,
    e.g. broccoli, carrots, mushrooms,
    peppers (capsicums), courgettes
    (zucchini), tomatoes

1 teaspoon sugar

salt and lemon pepper

30–50 g feta, or blue vein cheese

extra feta or blue vein for serving

Sweet pickled walnut spread

1 cup pickled walnuts

250 g cream cheese

Preheat the oven to 200°C.

Cut the ciabatta into slices about 2-cm thick. Allow 3 slices per person.

Drizzle each slice with garlic or olive oil, arrange on an oven tray and toast in the oven until golden and crunchy. Alternatively, drizzle with oil and toast on a barbecue hot plate.

Heat the cooking oil in a frying pan and add the garlic. Cook for a moment then add the vegetables and stir fry briefly — the vegetables should remain crisp.

Stir in sugar and season to taste with salt and lemon pepper. Gently crumble the feta or blue vein into the vegetables and toss together well.

To make the walnut spread, place the walnuts and cream cheese into a food processor or blender and process until smooth.

Serve the vegetables with extra crumbled feta or blue vein, bruschetta and a dish of sweet pickled walnut spread alongside.

The Pickled Walnut, Tolaga Bay, East Cape

Warm cumin lamb salad with blue cheese dressing

SERVES 4 AS A MAIN COURSE

Cumin rub
4 teaspoons ground cumin
2 teaspoons ground coriander
2 teaspoons sumac
salt and pepper

Lamb
4 small lamb rumps, trimmed of sinew
oil for frying

Vegetables
about 3 tablespoons extra virgin olive oil
1 eggplant (aubergine), finely chopped
baby cos lettuce leaves for serving
handful of toasted walnut pieces

Blue cheese dressing
1 kg natural unsweetened yoghurt
grated zest of 1 lemon
crumbled blue cheese to taste
salt and pepper

To make the cumin rub, mix the spices together and season to taste.

To prepare the lamb, preheat the oven to 200°C.
   Roll the lamb rumps in the cumin rub mix.
   Heat the oil in a heavy-based frying pan until very hot, then quickly sear the lamb rumps all over (about 2 minutes each side). Transfer to an ovenproof dish and roast until cooked medium–rare. Set aside to rest in a warm place before slicing.
   Heat the extra virgin olive oil in a frying pan and sauté the eggplant until golden.

To make the blue cheese dressing, place the yoghurt into a bowl and whisk in the lemon juice, blue cheese and season to taste.

To serve, arrange the baby cos lettuce on large plates, top with a scattering of eggplant and slices of lamb. Drizzle blue cheese dressing over and arrange walnuts on the side.

Refrigerate leftover dressing in a well-sealed container for 1 week and use to dress any salad or as a dip for breads.

The Wharf Bar, Gisborne, East Coast

Gisborne city, on Poverty Bay at the mouth of the Turanganui River, is the centre of a rich crop, fruit and grape growing region and a popular destination for visiting pleasure craft.

Sugar-cured duck and lentil dolmades with artichoke salad and chilli yoghurt

SERVES 4 AS AN ENTRÉE

Sugar-cured duck

2 duck legs

⅛ cup rock salt

⅛ cup sugar

500 ml pomace oil

Dolmades

30 g red lentils

12–16 vine leaves

90 g rice

oil for frying

1 spring onion, chopped

1 teaspoon ground coriander

¼ teaspoon turmeric

200 g shredded sugar-cured duck

few strands of saffron

3½ tablespoons vegetable stock

juice of 1 lemon

1 tablespoon brown sugar

4 fresh dates, pitted and chopped

½ cup chopped fresh coriander leaves

salt and pepper

Artichoke salad

1 jar artichokes in oil

red onion, peeled and finely sliced

½ cup fresh flat-leaf parsley

2 shallots, finely sliced

1 tablespoon dukkah

100 g rocket leaves

Chilli yoghurt

250 ml thick Greek yoghurt

2 fresh chillies, deseeded and minced

¼ cup chopped fresh coriander leaves

lemon juice

To make the sugar-cured duck, trim the legs of any excess fat and rub the salt and sugar into the flesh and skin. Cover with plastic food wrap and leave to cure for 2 days in the refrigerator.

After 2 days, preheat the oven to 120°C.

Wipe off any excess salt and sugar mixture and place the duck in the bottom of an ovenproof dish. Pour over enough pomace oil to just cover the duck and bake for 2 hours until very tender with the flesh falling away from the bone. Shred the meat.

To make the dolmades, bring a large saucepan of water to the boil and cook the lentils for 15–20 minutes until just cooked.

Rinse the vine leaves and steam until tender.

Wash the rice and cook until al dente.

Heat the oil in a large frying pan and sauté the rice and lentils for 2 minutes. Add the spring onion, coriander and turmeric and sauté until fragrant. Add the duck and saffron and cook for 5 minutes. Pour in the vegetable stock and bring to the boil, then reduce the heat and cook gently until all the liquid is absorbed. Add the lemon juice, sugar, dates and coriander and season to taste.

Place a tablespoon of the mixture in each vine leaf, fold in the sides and roll up to make cigar shapes.

To make the artichoke salad, drain the artichokes and mix with the onion, parsley, shallots and dukkah and arrange on top of the rocket leaves.

To make the chilli yoghurt, mix all the ingredients together.

To serve, arrange salad on plates with 3–4 dolmades per person on top. To finish, drizzle around the chilli yoghurt.

Provedore, Napier, Hawke's Bay

Napier sits at the centre of a large scallop-shaped bay on the east coast.

Spicy chorizo-stuffed chicken Maryland with saffron risotto and roasted red pepper aïoli

SERVES 4 AS A MAIN COURSE

Stuffed chicken

4 whole chicken legs (Marylands)
2 chorizo sausages
2 red chillies, deseeded and chopped
2 cloves garlic, peeled and roughly
    chopped
1 teaspoon ground cumin
1 teaspoon ground coriander
2 egg yolks
salt and pepper
chicken stock or salted water for poaching

Red pepper aïoli

1 red pepper (capsicum)
a little olive oil for roasting
1 tablespoon wholegrain mustard
2 cloves garlic, peeled and roughly
    chopped
2 egg yolks
3½ tablespoons white wine vinegar
250 ml canola oil
salt and pepper

Saffron risotto

1 tablespoon butter
½ onion, peeled and finely chopped
2 cloves garlic, peeled and chopped
100 g arborio rice
5 saffron strands
300 ml chicken stock
2 tablespoons freshly grated
    Parmesan cheese
3½ tablespoons cream
salt and pepper

fresh herbs or mesclun for garnishing

To prepare the chicken, debone the chicken legs (or have your butcher do this for you) and place on a board skin-side down. Cover with plastic food wrap and gently flatten using a meat mallet.

Remove the skin from the sausages and place the meat into a food processor, along with the chilli, garlic, cumin, coriander and egg yolks. Purée until it forms a smooth paste, then season to taste.

Place one-quarter of the stuffing in the middle and along the length of each chicken leg (skin-side out), and wrap each leg tightly in plastic food wrap.

Fill a frying pan with enough chicken stock or salted water to cover the legs and bring to the boil. Reduce the heat until the liquid is just simmering, and poach the chicken until just cooked, about 15 minutes.

Preheat the oven to 180°C and carefully remove the plastic food wrap from the chicken. Transfer to a roasting dish and roast the chicken for about 10 minutes or until golden.

To make the red pepper aïoli, preheat the oven to 180°C.

Roast the pepper in a little olive oil until the skin blisters, remove from the oven and transfer to a plastic bag. Once it is cool enough to handle, remove the skin, stalk and seeds.

Place the roasted pepper, mustard, garlic and egg yolks into a food processor and purée, then add the vinegar and slowly add the oil with the motor running until the sauce is thickened. Season to taste.

To make the risotto, melt the butter in a heavy-based frying pan and gently sauté the onion and garlic until softened, taking care not to brown them. Add the rice and saffron and sauté, stirring continuously. Gradually add the stock, a little at a time, adding more as it is absorbed. Cook until the rice is al dente, then stir in the Parmesan and cream. Season to taste.

To serve, place large spoonfuls of risotto on plates. Slice each chicken leg into 4 pieces and arrange on the rice, then spoon over some red pepper aioli. Garnish with fresh herbs or mesclun.

Caution@Shed 2 and Bar, Napier, Hawke's Bay

Napier's Marine Parade, with its stately Norfolk Island pines, gardens, fountains and statuary, is one of New Zealand's premier seaside boulevards.

Scallops with Japanese salsa on Chinese spoons

MAKES 20

Japanese salsa

4 tomatoes, quartered, deseeded and
    finely diced

1 small telegraph cucumber, deseeded and
    finely diced

2 tablespoons pickled ginger, finely sliced

2 tablespoons sweet chilli sauce

1 tablespoon chopped fresh coriander

1 dessertspoon sesame oil

½ tablespoon fish sauce

juice of 1 lemon

good pinch of cracked pepper

Scallops

20 scallops

salt and pepper

grapeseed oil

20 x Chinese spoons for serving

To make the salsa, mix all the ingredients together in a bowl.

Place generous spoonfuls of salsa into the Chinese spoons.

To prepare the scallops, heat a heavy-based frying pan or a barbecue hotplate until very hot but not smoking.

Drain excess moisture from the scallops, season to taste and toss in grapeseed oil.

Sear both sides of the scallops for about 1 minute per side. They need to be soft to the touch. If using a frying pan, do not cook too many at once, or the scallops will stew.

Remove the scallops from the heat immediately and arrange 1 in each of the prepared spoons.

Alternatively, serve the scallops on warmed plates with the salsa spooned over.

Clearview Estate Winery Restaurant, Te Awanga, Hawke's Bay

Around the sunny city of Napier (above and opposite) are popular swimming and surfing beaches.

Pan-fried snapper on lemon and parsley crushed potatoes with avocado salsa

SERVES 4 AS A MAIN COURSE

Avocado salsa

6 avocados, peeled and roughly chopped
½ red onion, peeled and finely chopped
4 cloves garlic, peeled and crushed
3 tomatoes, deseeded, cored and diced
2 tablespoons chopped coriander
½ dessertspoon cracked black pepper
2 tablespoons sesame oil
1 tablespoon fish sauce
4–5 tablespoons sweet chilli sauce
juice of 3 lemons

Crushed potatoes

6 large Agria potatoes, scrubbed and
    peeled roughly (leaving some skin)
about 8 tablespoons extra virgin olive oil
zest and juice of 1 lemon
2 tablespoons chopped fresh flat-leaf
    parsley
salt and white pepper

Snapper

700–800 g snapper fillets (or other firm
    white fish), skin on
olive oil for frying
lemon or lime wedges for garnishing
handful of fresh rocket tossed in balsamic
    vinegar and extra virgin olive oil for
    garnishing

To make the avocado salsa, gently mix all the ingredients together. The salsa can be made the day before and stored in the refrigerator.

To make the crushed potatoes, bring the potatoes to the boil in a large saucepan of salted water and cook until tender. Tip into a colander and leave for a few minutes to drain well. Return the cooked potatoes to the pan and mash roughly. Stir in the olive oil, lemon zest and juice and parsley and season to taste.

To prepare the snapper, heat a large frying pan or the hot plate on a barbecue. Fry the fish, skin-side down, in a little olive oil for about 2 minutes. Turn the fish and lower the heat and continue to cook for a further 4 minutes (depending on the thickness of the fish) until just cooked.

Serve the fish immediately on the hot crushed potato. Arrange the avocado salsa on top and garnish with lemon or lime wedges and some dressed rocket.

Clearview Estate Winery Restaurant, Te Awanga, Hawke's Bay

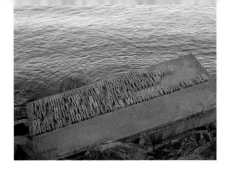

Sashimi plate

SERVES 4 AS AN ENTRÉE

Sashimi dressing (makes about 1 cup)

1 small onion, peeled and chopped

4 tablespoons soy sauce

3½ tablespoons rice vinegar

3½ tablespoons water

½ teaspoon sugar

sea salt and freshly ground black pepper

½ teaspoon mustard powder

1 tablespoon grapeseed oil

1 tablespoon sesame oil

Soy-sake sauce (makes about 1 cup)

2 litres water

190 g sugar

140 ml soy sauce

3½ tablespoons sake

Miso broth

50 g dried wakame seaweed

80 g firm tofu, diced

1 cup water

1 teaspoon bonito flakes

4 dried shitake mushrooms

1 tablespoon tamari

2 teaspoon blond miso paste

Pickled mushrooms

4 shitake mushrooms (reserved from the
    miso broth)

50 g oyster mushrooms

50 g snow needle mushrooms

50 g enokitake mushrooms

3 tablespoons sugar

2 tablespoons rice vinegar

1 tablespoons sake

Prawn and bok choy

1 bulb bok choy, steamed

8 Ama Ebi prawns (school prawns)

1 teaspoon Japanese preserved ginger,
    thinly sliced

To make the sashimi dressing, mix the onion, soy sauce, rice vinegar, water, sugar, salt, pepper and mustard powder together, then whisk in the oils.

Let the dressing rest for 30 minutes, then strain, discarding the onion. The dressing will keep for a week or so, refrigerated, if you don't use it all at once.

To make the soy-sake sauce, mix the water, sugar, soy sauce and sake together in a deep saucepan and place over a moderate heat. Bring to a gentle simmer, then reduce until thickened or when it coats the back of a spoon, about 30 minutes.

To prepare the miso broth, place the seaweed into cold water to rehydrate, then drain. Divide the tofu and seaweed between 4 x 60 ml sake cups and keep in a warm place.

Place the water into a saucepan and add the bonito flakes, shitake mushrooms and tamari and bring to the boil.

Take off the heat and remove the mushrooms (set aside for the mushroom pickle). Reheat the broth, but do not boil it. Place the miso in a small sieve and submerge the sieve in the broth. Using the back of a spoon, gently rub the miso into the broth. Pour the miso broth over the tofu and seaweed.

To prepare the pickled mushrooms, thinly slice the shiitake and oyster mushrooms and place into a small bowl with the snow needle and enokitake mushrooms. Gently toss them together. Place the sugar, vinegar and sake into a small saucepan and bring to the boil, then pour over the mushrooms. Leave to cool before refrigerating. The pickled mushrooms can be kept in the refrigerator for up to 1 month.

To prepare the prawn and bok choy, peel the 4 outer leaves from the bok choy bulb. Wrap 2 prawns tightly in each leaf and top with the preserved ginger.

To prepare the tuna, toss the soba noodles in the sesame oil and season lightly. Divide the noodles between 4 mini flax kete and gently lay the sliced tuna over the top.

To prepare the crab salad, divide the seaweed between 4 shot glasses, and top with the cooked crab meat, the soy-sake sauce and the caviar.

To prepare the white fish, make 4 layers of fish over the mushrooms and dot with caviar.

To prepare the salmon, marinate the fish in the sashimi dressing for 10 minutes. Place 4 small piles of seaweed on each plate and top with slices of salmon.

To assemble the platter, spread some wasabi on each serving plate, then arrange and a dish of tamari, a bowl of miso broth and a dish or spray bottle of ginger syrup on each plate. Follow with an oyster on each plate, along with a bok choy-wrapped prawn, tuna kete, crab salad shot glass, white fish, and marinated salmon.

Martin Bosley's Yacht Club Restaurant, Wellington

The Wellington Writers Walk (above), located on Wellington's waterfront, commemorates some of New Zealand's greatest writers.

Tuna

50 g soba noodles, cooked

1 teaspoon sesame oil

salt and pepper

60 g bigeye tuna, thinly sliced

Crab salad

4 teaspoons pickled wakame seaweed

4 teaspoons cooked crab meat, drained

4 teaspoons soy-sake sauce

4 teaspoons salmon caviar

White fish

60 g white fish, thinly sliced

4 teaspoons pickled mushrooms

2 teaspoons wasabi flying fish caviar

Marinated salmon

60 g salmon fillet, thinly sliced

2 tablespoons sashimi dressing

4 teaspoons wakame seaweed, rehydrated
in cold water and drained

To assemble

wasabi for serving

tamari for serving

4 tablespoons pickled ginger syrup for
serving

4 rock oysters, in the half shell

Salt and pepper squid with an Asian salad

SERVES 8 AS AN ENTRÉE

Salt and pepper mix

2 teaspoons Szechwan pepper

2 star anise

1 cinnamon stick

2 teaspoons coriander seeds

2 teaspoons dried red chilli powder

100 g sea salt flakes

300 g rice flour

Asian salad

1 cucumber, peeled into ribbons

1 red pepper (capsicum), deseeded
and sliced

1 red onion, peeled and sliced

1 spring onion

½ cup fresh mint sprigs

½ cup fresh coriander

¼ cup fresh Vietnamese mint

1 cup mung beans

Nahm jim dressing

4 bird's eye chillies

4 cloves garlic, peeled

4 coriander roots

75 ml lime juice

3½ tablespoons fish sauce

Squid

12 squid tubes

grapeseed oil for deep frying

sweet chilli sauce, Asian plum sauce or aïoli
for serving

To make the salt and pepper mix, place the Szechwan pepper, star anise, cinnamon stick, coriander seeds, chilli powder and salt flakes into a frying pan and dry fry for about 5 minutes until fragrant. Cool, then grind to a powder using a pestle and mortar. Place into a bowl and mix in the rice flour.

To make the Asian salad, place the cucumber, pepper, red onion, spring onion, fresh herbs and mung beans into a bowl and mix together.

To make the *nahm jim* dressing, place the chillies, garlic and coriander root into a pestle and mortar and grind until it forms a paste. Transfer to a bowl and whisk in the lime juice and fish sauce. (This dressing doesn't keep well, so needs to be used within a few days of making.)

Toss the dressing through the salad.

Clean the squid tubes and pat dry using absorbent kitchen paper. Slice into rings and dust with the salt and pepper mix.

Heat the oil in a wok.

Deep fry the squid in small batches for about 5 minutes until golden.

Arrange the salad on plates with the hot squid on top.

Serve with sweet chilli sauce, Asian plum sauce or aïoli.

Vista Café, Wellington

Heading east around Wellington's pretty harbour, Oriental Parade takes in vistas of house-studded hills and boat harbours.

Pan-fried risotto cakes with sautéed mushrooms, feta and green olive tapenade

SERVES 6 AS A MAIN COURSE

Risotto cakes

750 ml vegetable stock

¼ cup extra virgin olive oil

1 large onion, peeled and finely chopped

2 sticks celery, finely chopped

2 cups arborio rice

125 ml white wine

1 tablespoon butter

¼ cup freshly grated Parmesan cheese

salt and pepper

Olive tapenade

300 g pitted green olives

60 g capers

2 cloves garlic

zest and juice of 1 lemon

2 tablespoons brandy

¼ cup extra virgin olive oil

¼ cup vegetable oil

¼ cup chopped flat-leaf parsley

salt and pepper

Sautéed mushrooms

25 ml extra virgin olive oil

6 flat mushrooms, cleaned and peeled

2 cloves garlic, peeled and crushed

15 g butter

salt and pepper

50 g feta for serving

finely sliced red pepper (capsicum) and
    chopped fresh coriander (optional)
    for garnishing

To make the risotto cakes, gently heat the stock in a saucepan.

Heat the olive oil in another saucepan and gently sauté the onions and celery until softened and translucent.

Add the rice and increase the heat to moderate. Stir well to ensure the rice is well coated in oil, and fry until the grains of rice are translucent.

Add the wine and stir until it is all absorbed.

Add 1 ladle of hot stock, stirring constantly until the stock is absorbed. Repeat this with the remaining hot stock until the rice is cooked al dente – this will take about 15–20 minutes. Once the rice is cooked, reduce the heat and stir in the butter and Parmesan, and season to taste.

Turn the risotto out onto a baking tray to cool, poking a few holes in the rice to allow the steam to escape. Once the rice is cool enough to handle, mould into cakes using a ⅓-cup measure. Place into the refrigerator to chill.

To make the olive tapenade, finely chop the olives, capers and garlic and place in a bowl.

Add the lemon zest and juice, brandy, both oils and parsley. Mix together well and season to taste. Cover and refrigerate.

To prepare the mushrooms, heat the oil in a frying pan until smoking, then add the mushrooms and garlic and cook through. Once the mushrooms are cooked, place the butter on top and season to taste.

To serve, preheat the oven to 200°C.

Pan fry the risotto cakes in a little oil, then bake for about 8 minutes.

Place 2 risotto cakes on each plate, top with a mushroom, then crumble feta over the top. Spoon on some green olive tapenade and garnish with red pepper.

Soi Café and Bar, Wellington

Colourful boat sheds, yachts and bigger craft are part of the charms at Wellington harbour.

Nelson & Marlborough

New Zealand's Garden of Eden is the northern part of the South Island. From the golden Wither Hills in the east, across the Richmond Range to Tasman Bay and north to Cape Farewell, this area has everything in abundance, including unparallelled scenery and copious sunshine. The climate and soil combine to produce intensely flavoured apples, pears and berries, full-bodied grapes, contented animals and relaxed, happy locals.

Although laid-back, residents of Picton, Blenheim, Nelson and all the townships in between are seldom idle. There are so many outdoor pursuits in this part of the world, from caving and kayaking to mountain-biking, hiking and hunting.

The Marlborough Sounds, formed by ancient mountain ranges sinking into the sea, are a major drawcard. Winding waterways and sheltered bays – many of which can be reached only by boat – are home to more than 200 fish species, while several predator-free islands have become bird sanctuaries. Aquaculture is big business in this region, with nearby farms producing mussels, oysters, scallops and salmon.

Marlborough is New Zealand's largest grape-growing region – most notably Sauvignon Blanc, the aromatic and zesty wine variety that has found a place in the hearts of connoisseurs worldwide. The annual wine and food festival has grown from humble beginnings to a major showcase of local produce and culinary creativity. It's appropriate that Marlborough is also the centre of the country's sparkling wine industry. What better than a glass of bubbly to toast this paradise on earth?

Picton, at the head of Queen Charlotte Sound, is a fishing port and southern hub of inter-island shipping.

White chocolate and smoked apple cheesecake with Riesling verjuice syrup

SERVES 10

Smoked apple

500 g apples, peeled and cored

20 g soft brown sugar

20 g butter, cut into small cubes

Base

1 packet of your favourite plain biscuits

50 g melted butter

Filling

1 kg cream cheese

300 g caster sugar

400 g white chocolate

400 ml cream

3 eggs

Riesling verjuice syrup

500 ml Riesling verjuice

200 g sugar

seeds from 1 vanilla pod

2 star anise

1 cinnamon stick

whipped cream for serving

fresh mint for garnishing

icing sugar for dusting

It might seem like a lot of work to make smoked apples, but it is really easy and worth the effort! If you don't have a fish smoker you can use a gas barbecue. You will need wood chips, a wire rack and a lid (you could use an upturned stainless steel bowl for this). You don't need to use much heat to generate the smoke. The sugar and butter will counteract the bitterness from the smoke and the resulting flavour is stunning.

To smoke the apples, cut the peeled and cored apples into even-sized slices.
    Preheat the oven to 180°C.
    Arrange the slices in a stainless steel tray and sprinkle with the brown sugar and butter. Place into a fish smoker or on the barbecue and smoke until the butter melts, about 3–4 minutes. Remove the tray from the smoker and cover with aluminium foil. Transfer to the oven and roast for 5–6 minutes until the apple is just cooked, but still firm and not mushy. Set aside.

To make the base, place the biscuits into a food processor and process until crushed. Add the butter and continue to process until it all comes together. Press the crumbs into a well-greased 20-cm springform tin. Set aside.

To make the filling, preheat the oven to 120°C.
    Cut the smoked apple slices into chunks and arrange over the biscuit base.
    Combine the cream cheese and sugar.
    Place the white chocolate and cream into a saucepan and heat gently until the chocolate is melted. Beat the chocolate and cream into the cream cheese mixture, then stir in the eggs.
    Pour the mixture on top of the apple and biscuit base.
    Bake for about 2 hours until set. Once cooled, place in the refrigerator overnight.

To make the Riesling verjuice syrup, place the verjuice, sugar, vanilla seeds, star anise and cinnamon stick into a large saucepan and bring to the boil. Boil until the liquid reaches soft-ball stage.
    Set aside to cool.

To serve, arrange slices of the cheesecake on plates garnished with whipped cream and mint. Drizzle the verjuice syrup around the plate and dust with icing sugar.

Furneaux Lodge, Queen Charlotte Sound, Marlborough

The Marlborough Sounds is a labyrinth of idyllic intricate waterways.

Chargrilled aged sirloin with colcannon and tempura Marlborough oysters

SERVES 4 AS A MAIN COURSE

Colcannon

1 tablespoon duck fat

6 rashers streaky bacon, chopped

½ Savoy cabbage, finely chopped

salt and ground white pepper

about 4 cups mashed potatoes

2 spring onions, finely sliced

Sirloin

4 x 175–200 g aged sirloin steaks

freshly ground pepper and flaky
    Marlborough sea salt

Tempura batter

1 egg white

2 tablespoons plain flour

2 tablespoons cornflour

1 tablespoon very cold soda water

2 ice cubes

½ cup flour for dusting oysters before
    battering

oil for deep frying

8 fresh oysters

plain flour for dusting

1½ cups mixed micro herbs for garnishing

squeeze of fresh lime juice for serving

To prepare the colcannon, heat the duck fat in a lidded frying pan until liquid, add the bacon and sauté gently. Stir in the cabbage and cook for 15–20 minutes.

Remove from the heat, season to taste, cover and leave to stand.

Just before serving, heat the mashed potato and stir through the cabbage mixture along with the spring onions. Mix together well, cover and set aside.

To cook the steaks, season them to taste with pepper and sea salt. Heat the hotplate on the barbecue and cook them to your liking. Set the steaks aside in a warm place to rest.

While the steak is resting, prepare the tempura batter. Whisk the egg white to a soft peak and set aside.

In a separate bowl, sift the flour and cornflour together. Add the soda water and ice cubes to the flour mixture and mix in a criss-cross motion using thick wooden chopsticks. Gently fold in the egg white. Pour enough oil to fill a heavy-based frying pan two-thirds full.

Heat the oil, and drop in a little batter to test the temperature — the oil is ready when the batter floats back to the surface after dropping only halfway to the bottom. (If the batter reaches the bottom the oil is not hot enough.)

Dust the oysters with flour then dip them into the batter and slowly and gently place them in the hot oil. Move them around in the oil using a slotted spoon until they are cooked, about 1 minute each.

Remove from the oil as soon as they are cooked, drain and place on absorbent kitchen paper.

To serve, place the colcannon on plates. Arrange steak and oysters on top and garnish with micro herbs and a squeeze of fresh lime juice.

Bay of Many Coves Resort, Queen Charlotte Sound, Marlborough

The largest of the winding waterways in Marlborough is Queen Charlotte Sound. The vistas of water, hills and forest changes with every twist and turn.

Filo-wrapped Marlborough salmon on lemongrass risotto with tomato and coriander salsa

SERVES 6 AS A MAIN COURSE

Lemongrass risotto
2 tablespoons olive oil
1 onion, peeled and finely chopped
2 cloves garlic, peeled and finely chopped
2 teaspoons chopped lemongrass
450 g arborio rice
1.25–1.5 litres fish stock
2 tablespoons butter
handful of fresh flat-leaf parsley, chopped
50 g freshly grated Parmesan cheese
salt and pepper

Filo parcels
12 sheets filo pastry
100 g melted butter
6 x 170 g salmon fillets
about 60 g coriander pesto
salt and pepper

Ginger, lime and coriander dressing
1 cup freshly squeezed lime juice
1 cup palm or brown sugar
1 chilli, deseeded and roughly chopped
bunch of coriander, stalks and leaves,
    roughly chopped
2 tablespoons roughly chopped fresh
    ginger
1 stalk lemongrass, bruised and chopped
fish sauce

Tomato and coriander salsa
2 tomatoes, deseeded and finely diced
2 spring onions, finely chopped
3 tablespoons chopped fresh coriander
1 tablespoon lime juice
1 small red chilli, deseeded and sliced
salt and pepper

To make the lemongrass risotto, heat the oil in a heavy-based frying pan. Add the onion, garlic and lemongrass and sauté gently for 10 minutes until transparent and softened. Add the rice and stir until the rice is coated in oil. Reduce the heat to low and stir in 250 ml of stock. Allow the risotto to cook until the stock is almost completely absorbed before adding another 250 ml of stock. Continue to add stock and cook this way until the rice is al dente. Gently stir in the butter, parsley and Parmesan and season to taste.

To prepare the filo parcels, preheat the oven to 180°C.

Lay out a sheet of filo pastry and brush the surface with melted butter. Place another sheet on top and butter again. Lay a salmon fillet along 1 end of the pastry, spread a teaspoon of pesto along it, then season to taste. Wrap up the salmon in the pastry, folding in and buttering the edges. Brush the parcel with butter and place on a baking paper-lined tray.

Repeat with the remaining pastry and salmon fillets to make 6 parcels in total.

Bake the parcels for about 15 minutes until golden and cooked through.

To make the ginger, lime and coriander dressing, place the lime juice into a saucepan and bring to the boil. Remove from the heat and stir in the palm sugar until it dissolves. Add the chilli, coriander, ginger and lemongrass and leave to infuse for 60 minutes. Season to taste with fish sauce and strain before using.

To make the tomato and coriander salsa, mix together the tomato, spring onion, coriander, lime juice and chilli. Season to taste.

To serve, place generous spoonfuls of risotto on 6 plates. Cut the salmon filo parcels in half on an angle and arrange on the risotto with the salsa and dressing on the side. Drizzle ginger, lime and coriander dressing over the salsa.

Spinnaker, Waikawa Marina, Picton, Marlborough

Waikawa Marina at Picton, home to a fleet of pleasure and fishing craft.

Mussel chowder

SERVES 4–6 AS AN ENTRÉE

3 cups chicken or fish stock

1 cup dry white wine

4 tablespoons butter

1 onion, peeled and finely chopped

2–3 cloves garlic, peeled and crushed

1 red pepper (capsicum), deseeded and
finely chopped

1 carrot, finely chopped

2 potatoes, peeled and finely chopped

50 g plain flour

1.5 litres milk

sea salt and freshly ground black pepper

500 g fresh mussels, cleaned

1 tablespoon finely chopped flat-leaf
parsley for garnishing

Pour the stock into a saucepan and bring to the boil. Reduce the heat until the liquid is simmering, then add the wine.

Place the butter into a large, heavy-based saucepan, and melt over a medium heat. Add the onion and sauté gently until softened. Stir in the garlic, pepper, carrot and potato and cook for about 10 minutes, stirring frequently. Add the hot stock, simmer and reduce by one-third.

Mix the flour into the milk, then stir into the soup and continue cooking until thickened. Season to taste.

Steam the mussels until they are just opened, discarding any that do not open. Remove from their shells, leaving a few in their shells for serving. Chop roughly and stir through the chowder. Heat briefly.

Serve in bowls garnished with parsley and a mussel in the shell.

The Mussel Pot Restaurant, Havelock, Marlborough

The road from Picton to Havelock via Queen Charlotte Drive offers views over the scenic Mahau and Queen Charlotte Sounds.

Vine-ripened tomato tartare with olive tapenade, bocconcini and Alaskan king crab

SERVES 4 AS AN ENTRÉE

Olive tapenade

20 olives, pitted and coarsely chopped
handful of fresh flat-leaf parsley, coarsely
    chopped
1 tablespoon capers, rinsed, drained and
    chopped
1 teaspoon lemon juice
2 teaspoons olive oil
½ teaspoon anchovy paste (optional)
freshly cracked black pepper

Tomato tartare

2 vine-ripened tomatoes, deseeded and
    finely diced
2 teaspoons sundried tomato pesto
2 tablespoons freshly chopped flat-leaf
    parsley
salt and pepper

4 Alaskan crab legs, defrosted
2 bocconcini balls, each sliced into 4
hemp oil for drizzling
fresh dill for garnishing

To make the tapenade, place the olives, parsley, capers, lemon juice, olive oil and anchovy paste (if using) into a food processor and process until smooth. Season to taste with the black pepper.

To make the tomato tartare, mix the tomatoes with the pesto and parsley and season to taste.

Half fill 4 round moulds with the tomato mixture and press down firmly. Fill the moulds with tapenade and press down firmly again.

To serve, carefully remove the moulds and arrange on individual plates with a crab leg alongside. Serve with slices of bocconcini, drizzle with hemp oil and garnish with dill.

The Boat Shed Café, Nelson

Nelson city has an ideal location on the tranquil waterfront in Tasman Bay.

Oven-roasted monkfish with miso, mushrooms and cha soba noodles

SERVES 4 AS A MAIN COURSE

40 g dried black and white fungus (cloud ear mushrooms)

40 g dried shitake mushrooms

500 ml water

40 g dashi granules

50 g miso paste

1 teaspoon mirin

160 g cha soba noodles

chilli oil for drizzling

light sesame oil for frying

800 g monkfish fillets

12 tiger prawns, peeled (leave heads on) and deveined

2 bunches bok choy, well washed and roughly chopped

4 spring onions, sliced

Soak the dried mushrooms in warm water for 15 minutes. Drain and slice finely.

Place the water in a saucepan and bring to the boil. Add the dashi granules, miso paste, mirin and mushrooms and simmer for 5 minutes.

Bring another saucepan of salted water to the boil and cook the cha soba noodles, then drain and refresh. Drizzle chilli oil over.

Preheat the oven to 180°C.

Heat a little sesame oil in a heavy-based frying pan and sear the monkfish. Transfer to an ovenproof dish and roast briefly until cooked.

Just before the fish is cooked, add the prawns and bok choy to the simmering miso, cook for 2 minutes, then add the spring onions.

To serve, place the miso broth into bowls, arrange fish and prawns on top and serve the cha soba noodles hot or cold on the side.

Saltwater Café, Nelson

Nelson, as the centre of a vibrant forestry, fishing, horticulture and viticulture region, has a busy harbour and port.

Pan-fried salmon with mixed bean and walnut salad

SERVES 4 AS A MAIN COURSE

Walnut dressing

¼ cup walnuts, roasted

3½ tablespoons white balsamic vinegar

100 ml extra virgin olive oil

100 ml grapeseed oil

salt and pepper

Bean salad

1 cup green beans, trimmed

1 cup canned cannellini beans, rinsed and
    drained

1 cup broad beans, peeled

2 tomatoes, deseeded and finely chopped

sea salt

Salmon

800 g salmon fillet, skin on

olive oil for frying

To make the dressing, place the walnuts into a food processor and process briefly until chopped. Add the vinegar and oils and process until mixed. Season to taste.

To make the bean salad, blanch and refresh the green beans, then cut into thirds lengthways. Place the green beans into a bowl with the cannellini and broad beans and the tomatoes and add enough walnut dressing to cover them liberally.

To prepare the salmon, slice the salmon into 4 even-sized pieces. Heat a little oil in a frying pan and place the salmon skin-side down in the pan. Cook for about 4 minutes, then turn over and cook the other side for a further 2 minutes.

To serve, divide the bean salad equally between 4 plates and place the salmon on top, skin side up.

Orangerie Restaurant, Monaco Resort, Nelson

Batter

250 g self-raising flour
½ cup lager beer
1 cup cold water

Fritters

about 2–3 apples, peeled, cored and
    sliced into 12 rings
plain flour for dusting
grapeseed oil for deep frying
2 cups brown sugar
1 tablespoon cinnamon
maple syrup for serving
vanilla ice cream for serving
angelica sprigs for garnishing

Apple fritters

SERVES 4

To make the batter, whisk the flour, beer and water together until smooth.

Dust the apple rings with flour, then dip into the batter.

Heat the oil in a deep fryer or deep heavy-based frying pan. Drop in a little batter to test the temperature — the oil is ready when the batter floats back to the surface after dropping only halfway to the bottom (if the batter reaches the bottom the oil is not hot enough). Cook the apple fritters in the hot oil and remove with a slotted spoon.

Combine the brown sugar and cinnamon and use for tossing fritters.

Serve immediately, drizzled with maple syrup and with a scoop of vanilla ice cream. Garnish with a sprig of angelica.

Shed One Café & Bar, Mapua Wharf, Nelson

Marinade

½ cup soy sauce
1 teaspoon crushed chilli
1 tablespoon crushed garlic
3 tablespoons brown sugar
¼ cup canola oil

600 g lamb rump, sliced
olive oil for frying

Salad

about 3 tablespoons sweet chilli sauce,
    according to taste
2 tablespoons coriander pesto
2 tablespoons sesame oil
2 spring onions, finely chopped
1 red pepper (capsicum), deseeded and
    finely sliced
1 carrot, peeled and finely julienned
½ cup cherry tomatoes
8 small gourmet potatoes, cooked and
    halved
1–2 cups mesclun

Thai lamb salad

SERVES 4 AS A MAIN COURSE

To make the marinade, mix all the ingredients together in a bowl.

Add the lamb and set aside to marinate, covered in the refrigerator, for about 1 hour.

To make the salad, mix together the sweet chilli sauce, coriander pesto and sesame oil in a mixing bowl. Add the spring onion, red pepper, carrot, cherry tomato, potato and mesclun and toss together well. Set aside while you cook the lamb.

To cook the lamb, heat a little olive oil in a heavy-based frying pan and fry the lamb briefly on each side. Remove from heat and rest for 5–10 minutes.

Toss the lamb with the other salad ingredients and serve hot or cold.

Shed One Café & Bar, Mapua Wharf, Nelson

Smoked fish and manuka-smoked bacon with spinach and watercress cream

SERVES 4 AS A MAIN COURSE

Spinach and watercress cream
400 ml vegetable stock
400 ml cream
1 tablespoon chopped garlic
2 tablespoons cornflour
salt and pepper
a little freshly grated nutmeg
2 large handfuls of fresh spinach
1 handful of watercress
1 large dollop crème fraîche

mixture of fresh smoked fish fillets (salmon,
    warehou, tarakihi, cod or hake), trimmed
    into large 40 g portions (allow 3–4
    pieces per person)
4 rashers manuka-smoked bacon
8 potatoes, lightly steamed
fresh watercress for garnishing

To make the spinach and watercress cream, bring the stock, cream and garlic to the boil. Combine cornflour with a little cold water to make a paste and stir it into the cream. Simmer briefly until it thickens. Season to taste with the salt, pepper and nutmeg.

Remove from the heat and add the spinach, watercress and crème fraîche. Mix well with a wooden spoon, then transfer to a food processor. Process until the sauce is smooth and bright green. Adjust the seasonings if necessary.

Preheat the oven to 250°C.

Spray an ovenproof dish with non-stick cooking spray and place smoked fish portions in it, with the bacon rashers on top.

Heat for about 3–4 minutes or until the bacon starts to crisp.

To serve, place the warm potatoes into large serving bowls topped with the spinach cream sauce. Arrange smoked fish and bacon on top. Garnish with fresh watercress.

The Smokehouse Café and Bar, Mapua Wharf, Nelson

Mapua is a quiet coastal village alongside Rabbit Island, in Tasman Bay.

Goats' cheese and basil panna cotta with leeks, artichokes, pine nuts and pesto

SERVES 4 AS AN ENTRÉE

Panna cotta

100 ml cream

100 g feta

1 sheet gelatine

25 g fresh basil leaves, torn

salt and pepper

Pesto

100 g mixture of fresh basil and flat-leaf
    parsley

100 g pine nuts

120 g freshly grated Parmesan cheese

3 cloves garlic, peeled and chopped

250 ml olive oil

salt and pepper

1 baby leek, well washed

4 canned artichoke hearts in brine, drained

30 g pine nuts, toasted

To make the panna cotta, place the cream and feta into a saucepan and heat gently until the cheese has melted. Stir in the gelatine until it dissolves, add the shredded basil and season to taste.

Pour into 4 dariole moulds and place in the refrigerator for 2 hours until set.

To make the pesto, place the herbs, pine nuts, Parmesan, garlic and olive oil into a food processor or blender and process until smooth. Season to taste.

Peel the outer layers of the leek and slice thinly on a diagonal. Slice the artichokes into similar-sized pieces.

To serve, remove the panna cotta by running a hot knife around the inside of each mould. Place in the middle of a serving plate, and sprinkle the leek, artichokes and pine nuts around the outside of the panna cotta and drizzle with pesto.

Awaroa Lodge, Golden Bay, Nelson

In the South Island's north-western tip, Farwell Spit scribes an arc around Golden Bay, with the pretty inlet at Awaroa Bay (pictured) at its southern edge.

Slow-roasted venison steak with polenta and spicy poached pear

SERVES 4 AS A MAIN COURSE

Marinade
1½ tablespoons olive oil
4 cloves garlic, peeled and finely chopped
1 teaspoon smoked Spanish paprika
salt and pepper

4 x 200 g venison steaks
olive oil for frying

Polenta
640 ml chicken stock
250 g coarse cornmeal
80 g cream cheese
2 tablespoons freshly grated Parmesan

Herb butter
40 g butter, softened
3 cloves garlic, peeled and crushed
handful of fresh herbs, e.g. thyme, oregano,
    parsley, finely chopped
salt
1 tablespoon whisky or brandy (optional)
juice of ½ lemon

Poached pear
4 tablespoons sugar
about ½ cup water
2 whole red chillies, or to taste
2 star anise
2 pears, peeled, halved and cored
about 2 teaspoons sugar
about 20 g butter
2 teaspoons chunky cranberry sauce

Vegetable salad
600 g lightly steamed vegetables, e.g.
    courgettes (zucchini), carrots,
    green beans
40 g butter
2 tablespoons almonds, roughly chopped
2 tablespoons breadcrumbs

To prepare the marinade, mix together the olive oil, garlic and paprika. Season to taste and add the venison. Set aside to marinate, covered in the refrigerator, for 1–2 hours.

Preheat the oven to 80°C.

Place the marinated venison steaks into an ovenproof dish and roast for about 50 minutes or until the meat reaches a temperature of 55°C (test using a food thermometer). Remove from the oven.

Heat the olive oil in a heavy-based frying pan, or on a barbecue hot plate, then quickly sear the meat all over. Once it reaches 60°C (test using a food thermometer), the meat will be cooked medium–rare. If you prefer your meat more well-done, leave it for a little longer. Set aside to rest.

To make the polenta, preheat the oven to 180°C. Place the stock into a saucepan and bring to the boil. Pour in the cornmeal, stirring continuously, until very thick and you can stand a spoon in it. Stir in the cream cheese.

Spread the polenta onto a baking-paper-lined tray until about 2 cm thick. Set aside to cool. Sprinkle over the Parmesan and cook the polenta for about 30 minutes until golden brown. Set aside, and reheat before serving.

To make the herb butter, mix together the butter, garlic, herbs, salt, whisky or brandy (if using) and lemon juice. Form the butter into a sausage shape in plastic food wrap and store in the refrigerator. Cut into thin rounds before serving.

To make the poached pear, place the sugar into a saucepan and heat gently until it caramelises, then add the water and bring to the boil. Add the chillies, star anise and pear halves and cook until the fruit has just softened.

Heat a barbecue hotplate and sprinkle sugar over the cut side of the pears. Melt a little butter on the barbecue and brown the pears, cut-side down.

Remove from the heat and fill the hole where the core was with cranberry sauce.

Set aside, and reheat before serving, if desired.

To make the vegetable salad, steam the vegetables until just cooked.

Melt the butter in a frying pan, and gently fry the almonds and breadcrumbs until golden. Sprinkle over the vegetables.

To serve, arrange vegetable salad and hot venison on plates, with a slice of herb butter on top of the meat. Cut the polenta into wedges and serve with a poached pear half alongside. Garnish with fresh herbs.

Sans Souci Inn, Pohara Beach, Nelson

Pohara Beach (above), not far from Takaka on the shores of Golden Bay, is a popular destination for summer holidaymakers.

Kaikoura, West Coast & Canterbury

Known as a region of contrasts – snow-capped mountains, sun-parched plains, meandering rivers, roaring waterfalls, English heritage and French culture, scorching summers and freezing winters – from Kaikoura in the north-east to Caroline Bay in the south-east and Hokitika and Barrytown to the west, this is nature's adventure playground.

The Southern Alps offer year-round exhilaration for skiers, climbers and walkers, while both coastlines satisfy surfers, swimmers and boaties.

Kaikoura is a fantastic spot to watch a whale breach the water as it feeds. It's also a superb place to eat fresh crayfish – after all, the town's name means 'to eat crayfish'.

Further south, the Canterbury Plains are renowned for spring lamb but are also gaining a reputation for other meats, such as pork and venison, and newer culinary offerings, including gourmet cheeses, nuts, and even saffron. There is also a burgeoning wine industry in Waipara. All of this is good news for the chefs of Christchurch and nearby Akaroa, where French heritage dictates the importance of fresh produce and quality wines.

Across Arthur's Pass is the West Coast, a special part of the world where residents are keen to share with visitors their goldmining history, awesome glaciers, pancake rocks, wild beaches and ancient bush. The lasting impression inspires many to return again and again.

Kaikoura, set in its own beautiful bay, has long been a fishing town, but now whale watching and other sea mammal experiences are also available.

Salmon coulibiac

SERVES 4–6 AS A MAIN COURSE

2 red peppers (capsicums)
150 ml olive oil
8 Portobello mushrooms, sliced
4 courgettes (zucchini), sliced lengthways
1 eggplant (aubergine), sliced into
    10 mm rounds
8 sundried tomatoes, roughly chopped
salt and freshly ground black pepper
1 large sheet ready-made puff pastry
1 side of salmon, skinned and pin bones
    removed
100 g basil pesto
1 beaten egg yolk, for glazing

Preheat the oven to 180°C.

Place the red peppers in a roasting dish and drizzle with a little of the olive oil. Roast in the oven until the skin blisters, then set aside to cool. Once they are cool enough to handle, peel the skin, remove the stalk and seeds and slice finely.

Combine all vegetables, including roasted peppers, in a baking dish. Drizzle with the rest of the olive oil and season with salt and pepper. Place under a medium grill until just tender. Once finished, switch oven back to bake mode at 180°C.

To assemble the coulibiac, roll the pastry to form a large square, about 3–4 mm thick.

Place the salmon along the centre of the pastry. Spread pesto over one whole side of the salmon. Season with salt and pepper.

Layer the grilled vegetables on top of the salmon.

Fold the sides of the pastry over the filling and brush with beaten egg yolk. Sprinkle with sesame seeds.

Cook for 20–25 minutes or until the pastry is golden brown. Remove from the oven and set aside to cool. Once it is cool, slice ready for serving.

Serve the coulibiac hot or cold with aioli or lime mayonnaise, lemon wedges and salad.

Café Encounter, Kaikoura

The Kaikoura coast sits in front of the steeply rising foothills of the Seaward Kaikoura Range, snow-draped in winter.

Citrus delight

SERVES 8–10

Lime tart
1 block sweet short pastry
700 ml sweetened condensed milk
250 ml lime juice
zest of 2 limes
6 egg yolks

Lemon ice cream
175 ml lemon juice
250 g caster sugar
6 egg yolks
finely grated zest of 3 lemons
3 cups cream, lightly whipped

Spun sugar garnish
½ cup sugar
2 tablespoons water

Orange coulis
350 ml orange juice
½ cup sugar

To make the lime tart, preheat the oven to 180°C.

Grease a loose-bottomed tart tin, and roll out the pastry to fit. Press the pastry into the tart tin, trim the edges, then line the pastry with baking paper. Fill with dried beans or uncooked rice and bake the tart case for about 20 minutes. Remove the beans and baking paper and return to the oven for a further 5 minutes. Remove from the oven and set aside to cool.

Place the condensed milk, lime juice and zest into a bowl and mix together well. Add the egg yolks and beat until smooth.

Pour the mixture into the cooled tart case.

Bake for 10–15 minutes until it has set — it will just wobble when shaken lightly. Allow to cool before serving.

To make the lemon ice cream, place the lemon juice into a saucepan and heat until it has reduced by slightly more than half. Stir in the sugar and bring back to the boil.

Whisk the egg yolks and lemon zest together, then pour the simmering lemon syrup over the yolks while continuing to beat. Beat until the mixture is cool and very thick.

Fold the cream into the lemon mixture, place into a container and freeze until ready to serve.

To make the spun sugar garnish, place the sugar and water into a saucepan and bring to the boil. Boil until the colour begins to darken, then remove from the heat and let cool just until the bubbles have settled. Using a spoon, drizzle the syrup in patterns onto a creased, baking paper-lined tray and leave to cool. These can be made in advance and stored in an airtight container.

To make the orange coulis, place the juice and sugar into a saucepan and reduce until the consistency of honey. Cool.

Serve the tart and ice cream with the spun sugar garnish and orange coulis alongside.

White Morph Restaurant, Kaikoura

Fresh barbecued crayfish

SERVES 8 AS A MAIN COURSE

4 medium-sized fresh live crayfish

olive oil for frying

salt

½ cup chopped fresh flat-leaf parsley, mint and basil

4 tablespoons garlic butter

splash of lemon juice

8 slices fresh wholemeal bread

4 lettuce leaves

2 cups steamed long grain rice

sprigs of fresh mint for garnishing

nasturtium flowers for garnishing

lemon wedges for garnishing

Submerge the crayfish in fresh water for about 30 minutes before cooking.

Bring a large saucepan or stockpot of salted water to the boil, add the crayfish and simmer for 5 minutes, then remove from the water. Place in the refrigerator to chill.

Once the crayfish are cool enough to handle, split them in half lengthways.

Oil a barbecue hotplate, sprinkle over a little salt and turn on the heat.

Place the crayfish meat-side down and grill for 2 minutes on a medium heat.

Turn the crayfish over and grill for another 2 minutes.

Generously sprinkle over the herbs, garlic butter and lemon juice.

Arrange the bread, lettuce and rice on plates or platters and place crayfish on top. Garnish with mint, nasturtium and lemon wedges.

Kaikoura Seafood Barbecue, Kaikoura

Swirling bull kelp. Kaikoura features a dramatic setting of mountains and sea, with a rugged rocky coastline.

Vegetarian pizza

SERVES 4–6 AS A MAIN COURSE

1 x ready-made pizza base

1 cup freshly grated Parmesan

1 red onion, peeled and chopped

1 green pepper (capsicum), deseeded, finely sliced and soaked overnight in a little sweet chilli sauce and about ¼ cup red wine

1 red pepper (capsicum), deseeded, finely sliced and soaked overnight in a little sweet chilli sauce and ¼ cup red wine

about 2–3 tablespoons basil pesto

about 2–3 tablespoons sundried tomato pesto

2 tomatoes, thinly sliced

¼ cup chopped fresh mint

Preheat the oven to 220°C.

Sprinkle the Parmesan over the pizza base, then the red onion.

Strain the green and red peppers, and set the liquid aside. Arrange the peppers on the pizza.

Dot the 2 types of pesto on top, then cover with tomato slices and mint.

Slide the pizza onto a baking tray and cook on the bottom shelf of the oven for 30–35 minutes.

While the pizza is cooking, place the liquid from the peppers into a saucepan and bring to the boil. Simmer until the sauce is reduced and thick.

Serve the pizza hot, drizzled with the sauce.

Buffalo Café, Barrytown, West Coast

Wild, deserted beaches of rocks and pebbles, backed by bush-clad hills, are typical of the South Island's West Coast. Barrytown is a short drive from Punakaiki, famed for its Pancake Rocks.

Denver-leg venison with port wine sauce

SERVES 4 AS A MAIN COURSE

600 g Denver-leg venison, cut into small
    medallions about 8-mm thick
olive oil for frying
½ cup Madeira
¼ cup beef stock
2 tablespoons green peppercorns
2 tablespoons port wine jelly
salt and pepper
sliced red peppers (capsicums) and sprigs
    of rosemary for garnishing

Heat a little olive oil in a heavy-based frying pan and quickly fry several medallions at a time, for 1 minute on each side. Keep the steaks warm while you finish cooking the remaining meat.

When you have finished cooking the meat, deglaze the pan with the Madeira, then add the stock, peppercorns and jelly. Gently simmer until it has reduced to a thickish sauce and season to taste.

Return the meat to the pan to warm through, then serve.

Serve with sautéed potatoes or a potato mash and garnished with sliced pepper and rosemary sprigs.

Café de Paris, Hokitika, West Coast

The beauty of the West Coast's beaches can be enjoyed from the coast-hugging road from Westport south to Hokitika.

Chocolate custard and Baileys layered cheesecake

SERVES 6

Base
200 g butter
400 g malt biscuit crumbs
40 g ground cinnamon

Filling
400 g cream cheese
100 g icing sugar
400 ml Baileys
1 teaspoon gelatine
400 ml hot water
8 tablespoons grated milk chocolate

Topping
400 ml milk
80 g custard powder
4 tablespoons roasted slivered almonds
whipped cream for serving

Spun sugar garnish
½ cup sugar
2 tablespoons water

To make the base, melt the butter in a large saucepan, then mix in the biscuit crumbs and cinnamon. Grease 6 x 8 cm-diameter, 5 cm-high moulds or 1 x 25-cm springform tin thoroughly. Press the biscuit mixture into the bottom of the moulds or tin to about .5 cm thick. Place in the refrigerator to set. Any leftover base can be frozen for later use.

To make the filling, beat the cream cheese, icing sugar and Baileys together until there are no lumps, then set aside.

Dissolve the gelatine in the hot water and add to the cream cheese mixture, mixing well.

Pour the cream cheese mixture into the moulds or tin to about 2 cm deep.

Sprinkle 2 tablespoons of grated chocolate on top of each cream cheese layer, then refrigerate until set.

To make the topping, heat the milk until almost boiling, then slowly whisk in the custard powder, beating well to avoid lumps. Cook gently until thickened. Set aside to cool.

Pour the cooled custard over the grated chocolate layer, top with the slivered almonds and refrigerate until set.

To make the spun sugar garnish, place the sugar and water into a saucepan and bring to the boil. Boil until the colour begins to darken, then remove from the heat and let it cool just until the bubbles have settled. Using a spoon, drizzle the syrup in patterns onto a creased, baking paper-lined tray and leave to cool. These can be made in advance and stored in an airtight container.

Serve chilled with whipped cream.

Poseidon, Sumner, Christchurch

Sumner Beach is a popular local playground for Christchurch city-dwellers.

Braised pork hock with saffron potatoes, red cabbage and pickled pears

SERVES 4 AS A MAIN COURSE

4 boned pork hocks
salt and pepper

Stock
2 tablespoons oil
1 onion, peeled and chopped
1 carrot, peeled and finely chopped
1 stick celery
50 g tomato paste
3 star anise
1 cinnamon stick
2 sprigs thyme
10 peppercorns
1 cup red wine
1 litre chicken stock

Pickled pears
4 organic pears
1 litre cold water
½ cup white wine
½ cup white vinegar
a few strands of saffron
½ cup sugar
1 clove
1 cinnamon stick
1 fresh bay leaf

Red cabbage
100 ml olive oil
1 red onion, peeled and chopped
1 small red cabbage, finely sliced
250 g redcurrant jelly
2 cups red wine
100 g sugar

Saffron potatoes
500 g Agria potatoes
a few strands of saffron
50 g butter
salt and pepper

Cut the pork hocks in half lengthways, trimming off any excess skin. Season to taste.

Place each piece of pork in plastic food wrap and roll up tightly. Repeat with the remaining pork pieces until you have 8 parcels. Set aside.

To make the stock, heat the oil in a heavy-based frying pan. Add the onion, carrot and celery and sauté gently until softened and lightly coloured. Stir in the tomato paste, and cook for another minute, then add the star anise, cinnamon stick, thyme, peppercorns, wine and stock and bring to the boil. Boil for about 40 minutes.

Preheat the oven to 180°C.

Place the hocks (still in their plastic food wrap) into a large ovenproof dish and pour over the stock and vegetables. Cook for 4 hours, then remove from the oven and let the hocks cool in the stock. Once cool enough to handle, remove the hocks from the stock and refrigerate overnight.

Reduce the stock over a high heat until thickened, then strain and place the sauce in a container in the refrigerator.

To make the pickled pears, cut the fruit into quarters and remove the core.

Place them immediately into a saucepan with the cold water to prevent them browning. Add the wine, vinegar, saffron, sugar, clove, cinnamon stick and bay leaf and bring to the boil. Simmer for 4 minutes, then remove from the heat and set aside to cool.

Once the liquid is cool, remove the pears and transfer to an airtight container. Strain the stock and pour the liquid over the pears. Any leftover pears can be left in their liquid in an airtight container for up to 3 months.

To make the pickled red cabbage, place the oil into a large saucepan, add the red onion and cabbage and sauté gently until softened. Add the redcurrant jelly, wine and sugar and reduce gently until there is no more liquid, taking care not to burn the cabbage. Set aside and keep warm if using straight away or, if you prefer, the cabbage will keep for about 8 weeks stored in an airtight container in the refrigerator.

To make the saffron potatoes, cook the potatoes in a large saucepan of boiling, salted water until tender, drain and mash. Add the saffron, butter and salt and pepper to taste.

To serve, preheat the oven to 180°C.

Remove plastic food wrap from pork hocks. Reheat the pork hocks in the oven for about 30 minutes until they are hot. Add the pickled pears for the last 5 minutes so they warm through and caramelise. Reheat the red cabbage in a frying pan if you have prepared it in advance, and reheat the sauce.

Arrange the saffron potatoes on plates and place the pork hocks alongside with some pickled red cabbage. Drizzle some sauce over and garnish with the pickled pears.

Ma Maison Restaurant & Bar, Akaroa, Banks Peninsula

Confit duck with peppered havarti gnocchi, fennel and orange salad and a wine and bay leaf foam

SERVES 2 AS A MAIN COURSE

Confit duck

2 duck legs

rock salt

about 1–2 litres (4–8 cups) duck fat, rendered

1 bay leaf

few sprigs of thyme

Gnocchi

200 g dry mashed potatoes

60 g peppered havarti cheese, diced

1 egg yolk

a little plain flour

grapeseed oil for frying

White wine and bay leaf foam

100 ml white wine

3 bay leaves

5 peppercorns

100 ml chicken stock

100 ml cream

Salad

2 tablespoons shaved fennel

4 orange segments

2 tomatoes, peeled, deseeded and chopped

2 sprigs of watercress

handful of fresh herbs, roughly chopped

salt and pepper

For serving

4 baby carrots

2 tablespoons baby peas

100 ml beef stock

10 ml truffle oil

chervil for garnishing

To make the confit duck, rub the duck legs all over with rock salt and leave overnight, covered, in the refrigerator.

Preheat the oven to 120°C.

Wash off the salt in water. Heat a little duck fat in a heavy-based frying pan and sear the legs until golden.

Transfer the duck legs to a small ovenproof dish and add the bay leaf and thyme and pour over enough duck fat to cover the legs. Cover the dish and place in a water bath and bake for 2–3 hours.

To make the gnocchi, mix together the potatoes, cheese and egg yolk. Add a little flour and mix until the mixture does not stick to your hands. Roll into a 2-cm log and cut into 3-cm pieces, pinching gently as you cut them to size. Bring a large saucepan of salted water to the boil, reduce the heat until just simmering and drop in the gnocchi. Poach until they float to the surface, then remove with a slotted spoon.

Refresh in cold water.

Heat a little oil in a frying pan and gently sauté the gnocchi until golden.

To make the wine and bay leaf foam, place the wine, bay leaves and peppercorns into a saucepan. Bring to a gentle boil, then reduce by one-third. Add the chicken stock and reduce by half. Add 80 ml of the cream and reduce by one-third, then stir in the remaining cream. Strain and purée with a stick blender.

To make the salad, mix together the shaved fennel, orange, tomatoes, watercress and fresh herbs in a bowl. Season to taste.

Briefly blanch the carrots and peas, then refresh in cold water.

Put the beef stock into a saucepan and reduce by half to make a jus.

Add the truffle oil and whisk together.

To serve, arrange the gnocchi on plates alongside the peas and carrots. Top with salad and a duck leg and drizzle over truffle and beef jus. Serve the foam alongside and garnish with chervil.

Harbour 71, Akaroa, Banks Peninsula

The village of Akaroa on Banks Peninsula (above) was founded by French whalers in 1838.

Chai-scented panna cotta with saffron and anise-poached pears

SERVES 6

Panna cotta

1 tablespoon gelatine powder

50 ml white wine

375 ml cream

50 ml milk

75 ml chai syrup

seeds from 1 vanilla pod

100 g caster sugar

Poached pears

500 ml water

150 g sugar

squeeze of lemon juice

3 star anise

1 cinnamon stick

good pinch of saffron

3 pears, peeled, cored and quartered

Mini ginger snaps

60 g caster sugar

30 g butter

30 g golden syrup

30 g plain flour

good pinch of ground ginger

Lime sorbet

600 ml water

300 g sugar

zest of 2 limes

juice of 4 limes

30 g egg white, partially whipped

To make the panna cotta, dissolve the gelatine in the wine.

Place the cream, milk, chai syrup, vanilla seeds and caster sugar into a saucepan and warm over a medium heat until the sugar has dissolved. Stir in the gelatine and wine and mix gently, then remove from heat.

Strain the mixture and cool. Pour into 6 dariole moulds and leave to set overnight in the refrigerator.

To make the poached pears, place the water, sugar, lemon juice, star anise and cinnamon into a saucepan. Rub the saffron between your fingers to crush and add to the pan. Add the pears and bring gently to the boil, then poach until the pears are just softened.

Remove from the heat and leave to cool in the poaching liquid.

Once cool, remove the pears and either leave them cut as they are or dice or purée them.

Reduce the poaching liquid until thick and syrupy.

To make the ginger snaps, preheat the oven to 180°C.

Mix all the ingredients to a smooth paste, then shape into small walnut-sized pieces.

Place on a baking tray, allowing plenty of room between each biscuit, and bake for about 5 minutes or until they have spread out and turned golden in colour.

Remove from the oven and allow to cool slightly before shaping each biscuit around a dowel to achieve the desired shape.

To make the lime sorbet, bring the water and sugar to the boil in a small saucepan and simmer until it forms a syrup. Pour the syrup onto the combined zest and juice and set aside to cool.

Fold through the partially whipped egg whites and place in the freezer, churning regularly until frozen.

Just before serving, whisk the frozen mixture to break up the ice crystals.

To serve, unmould the panna cotta and serve with diced poached pears and saffron syrup.

Le Monde Restaurant and Wine Bar, Timaru, Canterbury

Many Canterbury beaches carry shingle washed down the many rivers threading their way across the plains from the Southern Alps.

Grilled lamb cutlets with tabbouleh salad and mint oil

SERVES 4 AS A MAIN COURSE

Mint oil

large handful of fresh mint

1 cup avocado oil

salt and pepper

3 tablespoons red wine

Tabbouleh salad

3 heaped tablespoons bulgur wheat

1–2 tablespoons mint oil

juice of ½ lemon

small handful of fresh flat-leaf parsley,
    chopped

8 cherry tomatoes

½ red onion, peeled and finely chopped

salt and pepper

Cashew paste

3 fresh chillies, deseeded and sliced

handful of fresh coriander

1 tablespoon olive oil

1 clove garlic, peeled and roasted

handful of cashew nuts, toasted

salt and pepper

Lamb

8 best-quality lamb cutlets

fresh mint leaves for garnishing

To make the mint oil, crush the mint in a pestle and mortar (alternatively, use a stick blender). Add a little of the avocado oil and a dash of salt and pepper to the mint as you crush.

Mix in the red wine, then stir in the remaining avocado oil and transfer to a glass bottle.

It is best to let the mint oil sit for at least a week — as time passes, the mint infuses into the oil. Always shake well before using.

To make the tabbouleh salad, place the bulgur wheat in a bowl and pour over enough boiling water to cover the wheat. Leave to sit for 25 minutes.

Stir in the mint oil and lemon juice and place in the refrigerator to cool.

When cool, stir through the parsley, cherry tomatoes and red onion. Toss well and season to taste.

To make the cashew paste, place the chillies, coriander, olive oil, garlic and cashew nuts into a pestle and mortar and crush until it forms a fine paste. Alternatively, purée in a blender or food processor. Season to taste.

Roughly crush the cashews then stir into the paste.

To prepare the lamb, trim all the excess fat from the cutlets.

Spread the cashew paste over both sides of each cutlet, and pan fry for about 3 minutes each side. Set aside to rest for at least 3 minutes.

To serve, arrange 2 lamb cutlets, hot or cold, onto a generous serving of tabbouleh salad. Drizzle some extra mint oil around the plate and garnish with fresh mint.

Ginger & Garlic, Caroline Bay, Timaru, Canterbury

121

KAIKOURA, WEST COAST AND CANTERBURY

Otago & Southland

Rugged, untouched and wild are all words that spring to mind when contemplating the southern parts of the South Island. The Waitaki River marks the northern coastal boundary of Otago in all its glory. Across the border at Wallace Beach is New Zealand's southernmost region, Southland (which includes Stewart Island/Rakiura), exuding an unspoiled beauty of its own. Otago and Southland locals are descended from robust stock and although hard work is a proud tradition, people in these parts are just as keen to play. Bush-walking, golf, mountain biking, kayaking, angling and bird-watching are popular pastimes, along with perennial favourites rugby and netball.

Central Otago, New Zealand's hottest, coldest and driest region, is fast becoming an exciting wine-growing area while continuing to supply many of the nation's most succulent apricots, cherries and nectarines. Along the coastline, people look to the ocean for their food. Blue cod and crayfish are abundant, and at a certain time of year, local Maori make for the headlands and islands around Rakiura to harvest titi (muttonbirds).

From the southernmost tip of the mainland come oysters that many proclaim to be the best in the world. They grow slowly in the pure, cold water of Foveaux Strait and are slurped down by the dozen during opening-and-eating races at the famous Bluff Oyster and Food festival.

To the west is Riverton, a town with a Bohemian feel and a fondness for delicious, nourishing organic produce. Nothing stands between Rakiura and Antarctica, but even on a bitterly cold day, dinner is served with warm southern hospitality. At the end of the earth, it's easy to feel on top of the world.

Moeraki Beach, south of Oamaru, is the site of the extraordinary spherical boulders, mostly eroded from nearby cliffs.

Whole baked blue cod with almond and caper brown butter sauce

SERVES 4 AS A MAIN COURSE

Baked cod

4 small whole blue cod, scaled, gutted and
    fins clipped (or 1 large fish for the table)
4 lemons, sliced
selection of freshly picked herbs (including
    bay leaves, parsley, lemon thyme, etc)
olive oil
salt and pepper

Brown butter sauce

200 g butter
juice of 2 lemons
3 tablespoons toasted slivered almonds
3 tablespoons capers
2 tablespoons chopped parsley
salt and pepper
crisp green salad for serving
boiled potatoes for serving
halved lemons for garnishing

Preheat the oven to 190°C.

Slash each fish on both sides towards the head to ensure it cooks evenly. Stuff the cavity with the lemon slices and herbs, drizzle with olive oil, season to taste and place in a baking dish.

Roast for about 15–20 minutes until just cooked, then set aside to rest for 5 minutes.

While the fish is resting, heat a stainless steel frying pan over a high heat. Once the pan is hot, add the butter and move around the pan to melt evenly. Cook the butter until it takes on a rich brown colour and has a nutty aroma.

Remove from the heat and add the lemon juice to stop the butter cooking further. Add the almonds, capers and parsley. Season to taste and pour the sauce over the fish while still bubbling.

Garnish with lemon slices.

This method and sauce is delicious with any whole baked fish and is best served with a crisp green salad, and boiled new season potatoes and lemon halves on the side.

Fleurs Place, Moeraki Village, Otago

Some of the Moeraki boulders contain fossilised dinosaur bones.

Almond and pear tart

SERVES 8

400 g sweet short pastry
200 g butter
250 g caster sugar
zest of 1 lemon
4 eggs, lightly beaten
3 tablespoons plain flour
2 cups ground almonds
3 pears, peeled, halved and cored
icing sugar for dusting
whipped cream for serving

Preheat the oven to 175°C.

Grease a 27-cm loose-bottomed tart tin and line with baking paper. Roll out the pastry on a lightly floured surface. Chill in the refrigerator until the pastry is hard.

Beat the butter, sugar and lemon zest together until smooth, creamy and pale. Beat in the eggs. Add the flour and mix well, then stir in the almonds.

Pour the mixture into the chilled pastry case. Arrange the pear halves, cut-side down, evenly on top of the almond mixture. Push the pears down a little.

Place in the oven and bake for about 45–60 minutes until the filling is well browned, puffed up and completely set. Remove from the oven and cool completely.

Dust with icing sugar, and serve wedges with whipped cream.

Steam Café, Oamaru, Otago

Among Oamaru's attractions are numerous blue penguins, which have established a colony in a former limestone quarry. At nearby beaches the much more secretive yellow-eyed penguin can also be seen.

Sautéed prawns and scallops with chilli cream sauce

SERVES 6 AS AN ENTRÉE

2 tablespoons butter
2 tablespoons olive oil
24 scallops
24 prawns, shelled, deveined and heads
    removed
1 tablespoon white wine
¼ cup cream
1 teaspoon sweet chilli sauce, more if you
    prefer
fresh baby salad greens for serving

Heat half the butter and oil in a heavy-based frying pan and sauté the scallops until just cooked. Set aside.

Heat the remaining butter and oil and sauté the prawns until just cooked. Set aside.

Stir the wine, cream and chilli sauce into the hot pan, then reduce quickly.

Pour the sauce over the scallops and prawns and serve immediately.

Serve with a salad of fresh baby greens.

BeachHouse Café and Bar, Riverton, Southland

Slow-paced Riverton, at the mouth of an estuary in Southland, was one of New Zealand's earliest settlements, dating from sealing and whaling days.

Braised pork loin with Vietnamese salad and noodle spring rolls

SERVES 6 AS A MAIN COURSE

1 kg pork loin

Spring rolls

125 g packet soba noodles

100 g cooked or canned shrimps

¼ cup freshly chopped coriander

salt and pepper

12 spring roll wrappers

1 egg white

vegetable oil for deep frying

Vietnamese salad

1 bunch rocket

1 small cucumber, finely sliced

1 carrot, peeled and finely julienned

1 cup shredded cabbage

Dressing

100 ml sesame oil

50 ml oyster sauce

100 ml soy sauce

50 ml balsamic vinegar

100 ml apple juice

To prepare the pork loin, preheat the oven to 180°C.

Tie up the pork loin using butcher's string (or have your butcher do this for you), place into a roasting dish and roast for 1 hour. Set aside to rest.

To make the spring rolls, cook the soba noodles according to the packet instructions and drain. Place the noodles into a bowl and add the shrimps and coriander and season to taste.

Lay the spring roll wrappers out on a work surface and brush with the egg whites. Arrange tablespoonfuls of the mixture down one side of the wrappers, fold the ends to enclose the mixture, then roll over the sides to create a fat cigar shape.

Deep fry the spring rolls until golden, then drain and set aside to keep warm.

To make the salad, place the rocket, cucumber, carrot and cabbage into a bowl and mix together well.

To make the dressing, whisk the sesame oil, oyster sauce, soy sauce and balsamic vinegar together and set aside.

Slice the pork and transfer to a lidded frying pan. Add the apple juice and any juices from the meat and heat through.

To serve, place the salad on plates and drizzle over a little dressing. Arrange pork slices on top, cut the spring rolls in half and place alongside. Drizzle over some more dressing and spoon over the apple and pork juices from the pan.

The Pavillion, Colac Bay, Southland

Colac Bay, not far from Riverton, is a popular Southland surfing and holiday spot.

Sunken treasure oysters

SERVES 1 AS AN ENTRÉE

a little olive oil for frying
1 rasher bacon, finely chopped
¼ orange pepper (capsicum), deseeded
    and finely chopped
¼ red onion, peeled and finely chopped
juice and zest of 1 lemon
dash of Worcestershire sauce
6 Bluff oysters, shells reserved
salt and pepper

Heat the olive oil in a frying pan and gently sauté the bacon, pepper and onion until softened and the onion is translucent.

Add the lemon zest and juice and Worcestershire sauce.

Remove from the heat and spoon over the oysters in the half shell. Season to taste.

Place under a hot grill until the oysters are warm, then serve immediately.

Drunken Sailor, Bluff, Southland

Bluff, Invercargill's port, is the home of fishing fleets and ferries to Stewart Island.

Roast muttonbird

SERVES 2 AS A MAIN COURSE

1 fresh muttonbird (titi or sooty shearwater)

Stuffing
1½ cups breadcrumbs
1 onion, peeled and finely chopped
½ carrot, grated
1 apple, grated
1 tablespoon chopped mixed fresh herbs
½ cup spicy apricot sauce
orange juice to moisten
salt and pepper

roasted vegetables and green salad
  for serving

Preheat the oven to 160°C.
  Cut the muttonbird halfway through on the breast-bone side. Gut and clean it.

To make the stuffing, mix together the breadcrumbs, onion, carrot, apple, herbs and apricot sauce. Add enough orange juice to moisten the stuffing and season to taste.
  Stuff the muttonbird and sew it together with a metal skewer.
  Place the muttonbird on a tray inside a roasting dish so the oil can run out without the bird sitting in it. Roast for 1½–2 hours, until cooked. Check by inserting a skewer – the juices must run clear with no hint of pink.
  Once cooked, cut the halves right through and serve with roasted vegetables and salad.

Church Hill Restaurant, Stewart Island/Rakiura

Penguin apple cake

SERVES 12

1 tablespoon brown sugar
1 tablespoon sherry or rum
1 kg cooked chopped apples
250 g butter, softened
250 g sugar
4 eggs
350 g plain flour
1 teaspoon baking powder
icing sugar for sprinkling
cinnamon for sprinkling
ice cream or cream for serving
toffee sauce for serving (optional)

Mix the brown sugar and sherry or rum into the apples and leave to marinate for at least 30 minutes.
  Preheat the oven to 190°C. Line a 25-cm round cake tin with baking paper.
  Place the butter, sugar and eggs into a cake mixer or food processor and process for at least 15 minutes. Add the flour and baking powder. Stir in the marinated apples. Mix together well and spoon into the prepared tin.
  Bake for 50–60 minutes, or until a skewer inserted into the cake comes out clean.
  Sprinkle with icing sugar and cinnamon and serve warm with ice cream or cream and toffee sauce, if using.

Church Hill Restaurant, Stewart Island/Rakiura

Glossary

Black rice powder
Flour made from finely ground black rice. Often used as a dusting powder and to thicken soups and stews.

Bonito flakes
Dried bonito flakes, known as *katsuo-bushi* in Japanese, are flakes of dried smoked bonito, a kind of tuna. Available from Asian and specialist food stores.

Cha soba noodles
Noodles made from buckwheat and plain flours and green tea powder which gives them a distinctive green colour.

Chai syrup
Chai first appeared in India when a mixture of tea, cinnamon, cloves and various other spices were brewed together and strained to produce a spicy and aromatic tea. Chai syrup is a sweetened liquid that can be added to hot milk to make chai latte or used in cooking. Available from some specialist food stores.

Dashi granules
Dashi is used as a basic stock in Japanese cooking, and is made by boiling dried seaweed and bonito. Instant dashi granules are available from Asian food stores and some specialist food stores.

Glucose syrup
Glucose syrup is made from the incomplete hydrolysis of starch. It is most commonly made from corn starch but can be made from other starches, such as wheat, rice and potatoes. Available from specialist chocolate and confectionery stores and some pharmacies.

Harissa
This North African chilli paste is salty and often flavoured with spices such as coriander and cumin along with garlic and olive oil. It can be very hot, but some varieties are made milder with the addition of tomato or roasted peppers. It is readily available in supermarkets and specialist food stores.

Haloumi cheese
Originating in Cyprus, this firmish cheese is made from stretched curd (cow's milk, sheep's milk, goat's milk or a blend) and has a texture rather like mozzarella. It can be eaten uncooked or cut into chunks and grilled or fried. Available from specialist food stores and some supermarkets.

Inverted sugar syrup
Inverted sugar syrup is a mixture of glucose and fructose obtained by the hydrolysis of sugar. Available from specialist chocolate and confectionery stores and some pharmacies.

Israeli couscous
Israeli couscous is much larger than regular couscous and is made from rolled semolina. It swells up and doubles in size when cooked. Cook it as you would pasta in boiling, salted water until al dente. Available from specialist food stores and many supermarkets.

Lime kelp seasoning
Lime kelp seasoning is a blend of natural kelp (seaweed), lime and other natural ingredients to produce a fresh lime-flavoured seasoning. Available from specialist food stores and some supermarkets.

Micro greens
These tiny and delicate salad greens, smaller than baby salad leaves, are popular with restaurant chefs as a garnish. They are available from some specialist food stores, or you can grow your own.

Miso paste
Miso pastes, made from fermented soya beans, salt and rice or barley, range in colour and pungency from white to dark brown. The longer the soya beans are fermented, the darker and stronger the miso. Available from Asian food stores and some supermarkets.

Morello cherries
Morello cherries are small, sour cherries with a sharp, tart flavour perfect for cooking. They are available dried, in jars or canned from specialist food stores.

Pomace oil
This is the lowest grade of olive oil approved for consumption, and is obtained by treating the olive residue or pomace from previous pressings with solvents to extract any residual oil.

Sango sprouts
Brightly coloured sango (or radish) sprouts are hot and spicy with a definite radish flavour. Available from some supermarkets and greengrocers, or you can sprout your own.

Sumac
Sumac is a dried powder made from ground sumac berries, which grow wild throughout the eastern Mediterranean. It has a pleasant, salty, lemony taste and is mildly astringent. Available from most supermarkets and specialist food stores.

Szechwan pepper
This dried peppercorn is used in five-spice powder and *shichimi togarashi*, a Japanese seven-flavour seasoning. The leaves have a citrus fragrance and are used to flavour vegetables and soups. Dry-roast the peppercorns in a small pan until fragrant, then crush using a mortar and pestle.

Vincotto
Vincotto is derived from cooking must (pulped grapes) that have been left to wither on the vines for 30 days. Once cooked, the must is reduced to one-fifth of its original volume and left to age in oak barrels for up to 4 years. The flavour is uniquely sweet and sour and is alcohol free. Available from specialist food stores.

Wakame seaweed
Wakame is a thin, stringy deep green seaweed, commonly used in Japanese and other Asian dishes. Wakame is generally sold dried, and is available from some supermarkets and specialist food stores.

Weights & Measures

The following amounts have been rounded up or down for convenience. All have been kitchen tested.

Metric to Imperial

10–15 g	½ oz		50–55 ml	2 fl oz
20 g	¾ oz		75 ml	3 fl oz
30 g	1 oz		100 ml	3 ½ fl oz
40 g	1 ½ oz		120 ml	4 fl oz
50–60 g	2 oz		150 ml	5 fl oz
75–85 g	3 oz		170 ml	6 fl oz
100 g	3 ½ oz		200 ml	7 fl oz
125 g	4 oz		225 ml	8 fl oz
150 g	5 oz		250 ml	8 ½ fl oz
175 g	6 oz		300 ml	10 fl oz
200 g	7 oz		400 ml	13 fl oz
225 g	8 oz		500 ml	17 fl oz
250 g	9 oz		600 ml	20 fl oz
300 g	10 ½ oz		750 ml	25 fl oz
350 g	12 oz		1 litre	34 fl oz
400 g	14 oz			
450 g	1 lb		**Please note:**	
500 g	1 lb 2 oz		a pint in the UK is 16 fl oz	
600 g	1 lb 5 oz		a pint in the USA is 20 fl oz	
750 g	1 lb 10 oz			
1 kg	2 lb 3 oz			

Baking Pan Sizes

Common square and rectangular baking pan sizes:

20 x 20 cm	8 x 8 inch
23 x 23 cm	9 x 9 inch
23 x 13 cm	9 x 5 inch loaf pan/tin

Common round baking pan sizes:

20 cm	8 inch
23 cm	9 inch
25 cm	10 inch

Oven Temperatures

Celsius	Fahrenheit	Gas Mark
120°	250°	1
150°	300°	2
160°	325°	3
180°	350°	4
190°	375°	5
200°	400°	6
220°	425°	7

Note also baking paper = non-stick baking parchment.
In New Zealand, South Africa, the UK and the USA
1 tablespoon equals 15 ml.
In Australia 1 tablespoon equals 20 ml.

Index

Italicised page numbers indicate recipe photographs

Directory of Restaurants & Cafés

Awaroa Lodge

Abel Tasman National Park
Nelson
Tel: 03-5288758
Email: chef@awaroalodge.co.nz
Website: www.awaroalodge.co.nz
Head chef: Kirsty Walker
Manager: Alan Forsdick

The Foredeck

Bay of Many Coves Resort
Queen Charlotte Sound
Tel: 03-5799771
Email: office@bayofmanycovesresort.co.nz
Website: www.bayofmanycovesresort.co.nz
Managers: Mark & Lisa Jensen

Beach House Café and Bar

126 Rocks Highway
Riverton
Tel: 03-2348274
Head chef: Jean Tuhiwai
Manager: Angela Guy

Boat Shed Café

350 Wakefield Quay
Nelson
Tel: 03-5469783
Email: aaron@boatshedcafe.co.nz
Website: www.boatshedcafe.co.nz
Head chef: Ryan Hewitt
Manager: Aaron McCorkindale

Buffalo Café & Bar

Coast Road, SH6
Barrytown, West Coast
Tel: 03-7311151
Head chef: Damian Hands

Café de Paris

19–21 Tancred Street
Hokitika
Tel: 03-7558933
Email: pesquilat@xtra.co.nz
Head chef: Trevor Esson
Manager: Pierre Esquilat

Café Encounter

Encounter Kaikoura
96 Esplanade, Kaikoura
Tel: 03-3196777
Email: info@encounterkaikoura.co.nz
Website: www.encounterkaikoura.co.nz
Head chef: Nigel Evans
Owners: Lynette & Dennis Buurman and
Ian Bradshaw
Manager: Meike Verschoor

Carrington Resort – A Heritage Hotel

Maitai Bay Road
Karikari Peninsula
Tel: 09-4087222
Email: info@carrington.co.nz
Website: www.carrington.co.nz
Head chef: Scott Fraser

Cathedral Cove Macadamias

335 Lees Road
Hahei, Coromandel
Tel: 07-8671221
Email: hamish@cathedralcovemacadamias.co.nz
Website: www.cathedralcovemacadamias.co.nz
Head chef/manager: Hamish Pilkington

Caution@Shed 2 & Bar

Cnr West Quay and Lever Street
Ahuriri, Napier
Tel: 06-8352202
Email: theshed@shed2.com
Website: www.shed2.co.nz
Head chef: Simon Bold
Manager: Dennis Buckley

Church Hill Restaurant

36 Kamahi Road
Stewart Island
Tel: 03-2191323
Email: greatfood@churchhillrestaurant.com
Website: www.churchhillrestaurant.com
Chefs/owners: Gary Huggins and Annett Eiselt

Clearview Estate Winery & Restaurant

194 Clifton Road
Te Awanga, Hawke's Bay
Tel: 06-8750150
Email: enquiries@clearviewestate.co.nz
Website: www.clearviewestate.co.nz
Head chef: Kerry MacKay
Owner/managers: Tim Turvey and Helma van
den Berg

Copthorne Hotel & Resort Hokianga

State Highway 12
Omapere, Northland
Tel: 09-4058737
Head chef: Matt Begbie
Owner: Shane Lloydd

Drunken Sailor

8 Ward Parade
Stirling Point, Bluff
Tel: 03-2128855
Email: drunkensailor@xtra.co.nz
Head chef: Mareeka Barrie
Owner: Lisa Vaughan

Eggsentric Café

1049 Purangi Road
Flaxmill Bay, Coromandel
Tel: 07-8660307
Email: eggsentric@xtra.co.nz
Website: www.eggsentric.co.nz
Head chef/manager: Dave Fowell

Fleurs Place

169 Haven Street
Moeraki Village
Tel: 03-4394480
Email: mail@fleursplace.co.nz
Website: www.fleursplace.co.nz
Head chef: Simon Peacock
Manager: Fleur Sullivan

Furneaux Lodge

Endeavour Inlet
Queen Charlotte Sound
Marlborough
Tel: 03-5798259
Email: info@furneaux.co.nz
Website: www.furneaux.co.nz
Executive chef: Stuart Cliffin
Manager: Geoffrey Faulkner

Gannets International Feeding Ground

Corner York & Chapel Streets
Russell, Bay of Islands
Tel: 09-4037990
Email: njoy@gannets.co.nz
Website: www.gannets.co.nz
Manager/head chef: Rene Stumpp

Ginger & Garlic Restaurant

335 Stafford Street
Timaru
Tel: 03-6883981
Email: kerina@gingerandgarlic.co.nz
Website: gingerandgarlic.co.nz
Hosts: Jason & Kerina Cleverley

Hammerheads Restaurant & Bar

19 Tamaki Drive
Okahu Bay, Auckland
Tel: 09-5214400
Email: info@hammerheads.co.nz
Website: www.hammerheads.co.nz
Executive chef: Darren Gallagher
Manager: Paula Sheahan

Harbour 71 Restaurant & Bar

71 Beach Road
Akaroa, Banks Peninsula
Tel: 03-3047656
Email: l.dwright@xtra.co.nz
Chefs/managers: Darren & Leanne Wright

Harbourside Seafood Bar & Grill

First Floor, Ferry Buildings
Quay Street, Auckland
Tel: 09-3070486
Email: harbourside.auck@xtra.co.nz
Website: www.harboursiderestaurant.co.nz
Head chef: Phill Spathis
General Manager: Jeff Hamer

Hot Waves Café

8 Pye Place
Hot Water Beach
Coromandel Peninsula
Tel: 07-8663887
Email: hotwavescafe@paradise.net.nz
Head chef/manager: Mary Channings

Kaikoura Seafood BBQ

Jimmy Armers Beach
Seal Colony, Kaikoura
Tel: 03-3195389
Head chef/owner: Kathryn Claridge

Kamakura

29 The Strand
Russell Waterfront, Bay of Islands
Tel: 09-4037878
Email: contact@kamakura.co.nz
Website: www.kamakura.co.nz
Head chef:
Managers: Todd & Roberta Welling

Kestrel at the Landing

Water's Edge
120 The Strand, Tauranga
Tel: 07-9281123
Email: sue@thekestrel.co.nz
Website: www.thekestrel.co.nz
Manager: Sue Dyke

Le Monde Restaurant & Wine Bar

64 The Bay Hill
Timaru
Tel: 03-6888550
Email: le-monde@xtra.co.nz
Head chef/owner: Lindsay Bennett

Long Bay Restaurant

Long Bay Regional Park (on the beach)
Long Bay, North Shore, Auckland
Tel: 09-4735436
Email: andy_meyers@yahoo.com
Website: www.longbayrestaurant.co.nz
Head chef/ manager: Andrew Meyers

Ma Maison Restaurant & Bar

2 Rue Jolie
Akaroa, Banks Peninsula
Tel: 03-3047668
Email: mamaison@ihug.co.nz
Website: www.mamaison.co.nz
Head chef/owner: Rod Parkinson

Martin Bosley's Yacht Club Restaurant

103 Oriental Parade
Wellington
Tel: 04-9208302
Email: office.mbycr@actrix.co.nz
Website: www.martin-bosley.com
Head chef/owner: Martin Bosley

Mikano Restaurant

1 Solent Street
Mechanics Bay, Auckland
Tel: 09-3099514
Email: enquiries@mikano.co.nz
Website: www.mikano.co.nz
Head chef: John Flack
General Manager: Delvene Morrissey

Mudbrick Vineyard & Restaurant

Church Bay Road
Waiheke Island
Tel: 09-3729050
Email: info@mudbrick.co.nz
Website: www.mudbrick.co.nz
Head chef: Kevin Morgan
Manager: Nick Jones

The Mussel Pot Restaurant

73 Main Road
Havelock, Marlborough
Tel: 03-5742824
Email: musselpot@xtra.co.nz
Website: www.themusselpot.co.nz
Head chef: Laura Bell
Manager: Hannah Lucas

Okurukuru Winery

738 Surf Highway 45
New Plymouth
Tel: 06-7510787
Email: okurukuru@xtra.co.nz
Website: www.okurukuru.co.nz
Head chef/co-manager: Simon Houghton

Orangerie Restaurant, Monaco Resort

6 Point Road
Monaco, Nelson
Tel: 03-5470792
Email: theorangerie@monacoresort.co.nz
Website: www.monacoresort.co.nz
Head chef: Neil Ward
General Manager: Clare Davies

The Pavilion

188 Foreshore Road
Colac Bay, Western Southland
Tel: 03-2348445
Email: j.guise@woosh.co.nz
Head chef: Dave Winter
Owner: Julie Guise

The Pickled Walnut

43 Cook Street
Tolaga Bay, East Coast
Tel: 06-8626691
Email: thepickledwalnut@gmail.com
Manager: Meriana Thompson

Poseidon Restaurant & Bar

25 Esplanade
Sumner, Christchurch
Tel: 03-3267021
Email: poseidonrest@xtra.co.nz
Website: www.poseidonrestaurant.co.nz
Head chef: Brent Liley
Manager: Tom van der Spek

Provedore

60 West Quay
Ahuriri, Napier
Tel: 06-8340189
Email: mail@provedore.co.nz
Head chef: Zana Downie
Owners: Simon Kerr & Jen Cho

Pure Tastes

116 Marsden Road
Paihia, Bay of Islands
Tel: 09-4028448
Email: info@puretastes.co.nz
Website: www.puretastes.co.nz
Head chef: Tobias Wilkinson
Manager: Paul Jobin

Salt on the Waterfront

The Waterfront Hotel
1 Egmont Street, New Plymouth
Tel: 06-7695301
Email: sueandneil@waterfront.co.nz
Website: www.waterfront.co.nz
Head chef: Craig Stewart
Manager: Sue Drought

Salt Restaurant and Bar

1 Blacksmith Lane
Whitianga, Coromandel
Tel: 07-8665818
Email: dave@whitiangahotel.co.nz
Website: www.whitiangahotel.co.nz
Head chef: Bert van de Steeg
Manager: Dave Simmonds

Saltwater Café & Bar

272 Wakefield Quay
Nelson
Tel: 03-5483361
Email: saltwatercafe@xtra.co.nz
Website: www.saltwatercafe.co.nz
Head chef: Manfred Dax
Managers: Thomas and Vivienne Fox

Sans Souci Inn

11 Richmond Road
Pohara, Golden Bay
Tel: 03-5258663
Email: reto@sanssouciinn.co.nz
Website: www.sanssouciinn.co.nz
Chef/owner: Reto Balzer

The Sebel Trinity Wharf Tauranga

51 Dive Crescent
Tauranga
Tel: 07-5778704
Email: halo@sebel.tauranga.co.nz
Head chef: Daniel Simpson
General Manager: Gary Dickman

Shed One Café & Bar

Shed 1
Mapua Wharf, Nelson
Tel: 03-5402028
Email: shed1@shed1.co.nz
Head chef: Jamie Rouse
Manager: Marie Rouse

Slowfish Beachfront Café

Tower One
2 Marine Parade, Mount Maunganui
Tel: 07-5742949
Email: slowfish@wave.co.nz
Website: www.slowfish.co.nz
Head chef: Josh Ben-Chabat
Manager: Brigitte van Weele

The Smokehouse Café & Bar

Shed 3
Mapua Wharf, Nelson
Tel: 03-5402280
Email: smokehouse@iconz.co.nz
Website: www.smokehouse.co.nz
Head chef: Keith Stone
Owners: David Endersby & Julina Ismail

Soi Café Bar

Greta Point Wharf
305 Evans Bay Parade, Wellington
Email: dine@soicafebar.co.nz
Website: www.soicafebar.co.nz
Restaurateur: Brent Wong

Soul Bar & Bistro

Viaduct Harbour
Auckland
Tel: 09-3567249
Email: chef@soulsearch.co.nz
Website: www.soulbar.co.nz
Head chef: Gareth Stewart
Owner: Judith Tabron

Spinnaker Restaurant

Beach Road
Waikawa Marina, Picton
Tel: 03-5739152
Email: info@spinnakerwaikawa.co.nz
Website: www.spinnakerwaikawa.co.nz
Chef/owner: Hilary Weaver

Steam Café

7 Thames Street
Oamaru
Tel: 03-4343344
Email: tonimc@vodafone.net.nz
Chef/owner: Toni McLennan

Te Whau Vineyard & Restaurant

218 Te Whau Drive
Waiheke Island
Tel: 09-3727191
Email: info@tewhau.com
Website: www.tewhau.com
Head chef: Marco Edwardes
Owners: Tony and Moira Forsyth

Vista Café

106 Oriental Parade
Wellington
Tel: 04-3857724
Email: vistacafe@xtra.co.nz
Website: www.vistacafe.co.nz
Chef/owner: Dale Keith

Waikokopu Café

National Treaty Grounds
Tau Henare Drive
Waitangi, Bay of Islands
Tel: 09-4026275
Email: waikokopucafe@xtra.co.nz
Chef/owner: Hughie Blues

The Wharf Café, Bar & Restaurant

60 The Esplanade
Gisborne
Tel: 06-8684876
Email: lew@wharfbar.co.nz
Website: www.wharfbar.co.nz
Head chef: Kevin Murphy
Manager: Llewellyn Williams

White Morph Restaurant

94 Esplanade
Kaikoura
Tel: 03-3195676
Email: camber@ts.co.nz
Website: www.whitemorph.co.nz
Chef/owner: Gary Ford
Manager: Kerry Ford

Acknowledgements

As the production of this book got underway, it became obvious to me that without the dedicated help of a core group, the project would have been much less enjoyable. Louise Armstrong, Belinda Cooke and the team from New Holland have helped, cajoled and facilitated me on my way around the country. Without their assistance I'd probably still be in Akaroa or Russell. (Not that that would necessarily be a bad thing. I can think of far worse places to be stuck!)

The chefs and owners of the cafés and restaurants that I visited were incredibly accommodating and understanding of my tight schedule. Especially as the photographic shoots took place during their busiest season.

My daughter Harriet accompanied me on the complete circuit of the South Island and did a fabulous job of providing great company, carrying equipment and assisting in setting up the lights for the food photography. Of course I must also thank our other two family members, Trina and Katie, who kept everything running smoothly at home and put up with daily reports on both the amazing meals we ate and the stunning beauty of the places we visited.

Ian Batchelor

MAKING THE GRADE · GRADE 3

EASY POPULAR PIECES FOR YOUNG FLAUTISTS. SELECTED AND ARRANGED BY JERRY LANNING. EDITED BY MARTIN FRITH

FLUTE PART

Exclusive Distributors:
Music Sales Limited
Newmarket Road, Bury St. Edmunds, Suffolk IP33 3YB.
This book © copyright 1992 Chester Music.
ISBN 0-7119-2917-3
Order No. CH60006
Cover designed by Pemberton and Whitefoord
Typeset by Pemberton and Whitefoord
Printed in the United Kingdom by
Caligraving Limited, Thetford, Norfolk.

Chester Music

(A division of Music Sales Limited)
8/9 Frith Street, London W1V 5TZ.

THE INCREDIBLE HULK (THEME FROM)

Composed by Joe Harnell.

This theme from the TV series is a wistful and attractive melody, which reflects the gentle side of the Hulk's nature.

Try not to cut any phrases short before you breathe.

YESTERDAY

Words & Music by John Lennon & Paul McCartney.

Most peoples' favourite Beatles song. Notice the F sharp and G sharp in the ascending scale of A melodic minor (bar 4), followed by the F and G naturals in the descending scale.

EL CONDOR PASA (IF I COULD)

Musical Arrangement by J. Milchberg & D. Robles. English Lyric by Paul Simon.

This is a traditional melody from South America, made popular by Simon and Garfunkel.

Keep a very steady tempo.

SUMMERTIME

Music by George Gershwin.

'Summertime' is probably Gershwin's most famous tune. The notes aren't difficult,
but be careful that you play the correct rhythm in bars 11 and 12. Don't let the final D go flat.

ITSY BITSY, TEENIE WEENIE, YELLOW POLKADOT BIKINI

Words & Music by Lee Pockriss & Paul J. Vance.

If you want to leave out the spoken sections, you can cut from the first beat of bar 10 to the second beat of bar 12, and cut bar 22 completely. Watch out for the $\frac{2}{4}$ bar.

BRIDGE OVER TROUBLED WATER

Words & Music by Paul Simon.

Here is Paul Simon's most enduring song.

Try for a full, rounded tone as the piece builds to a climax around bar 23.

JEANIE WITH THE LIGHT BROWN HAIR

Words & Music by Stephen Foster.

This song needs really expressive playing.

Be particularly careful of the slurred ninth (A to B) in bar 14. The B should be really soft.

I KNOW HIM SO WELL

Words & Music by Benny Andersson, Tim Rice & Bjorn Ulvaeus.

Many of the notes are slurred in pairs,

which should be practised carefully to ensure that the second note of each pair 'speaks' clearly.

BIRDIE SONG / BIRDIE DANCE

Words & Music by Werner Thomas & Terry Rendall.

Articulate the quavers in the first section clearly, almost *staccato*,
to contrast with the smoothly phrased second part.

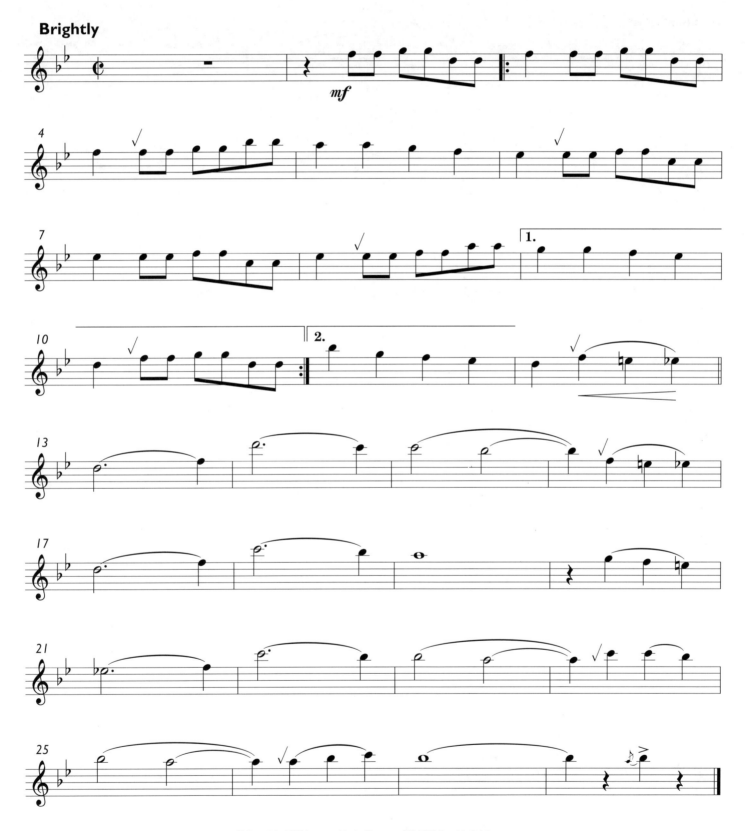

HE AIN'T HEAVY HE'S MY BROTHER

Words by Bob Russell. Music by Bobby Scott.

Some of the rhythms are a bit tricky in this piece. If you have some trouble with them,
practise each phrase slightly slower, counting in quavers. Be careful to count the rests in bar 21.

AMERICA

Music by Leonard Bernstein. Lyrics by Stephen Sondheim.

In this lively number from 'West Side Story' the time signature alternates between $\frac{6}{8}$ and $\frac{3}{4}$; you will need to keep this clearly in mind in bars 17 to 25.

BERGERAC

Composed by George Fenton.

Another TV theme, which here makes a substantial concert piece. The main theme is repeated an octave higher.

Remember that D. 𝄋 al ⊕ Coda means 'Go back to the sign, then take the coda'.

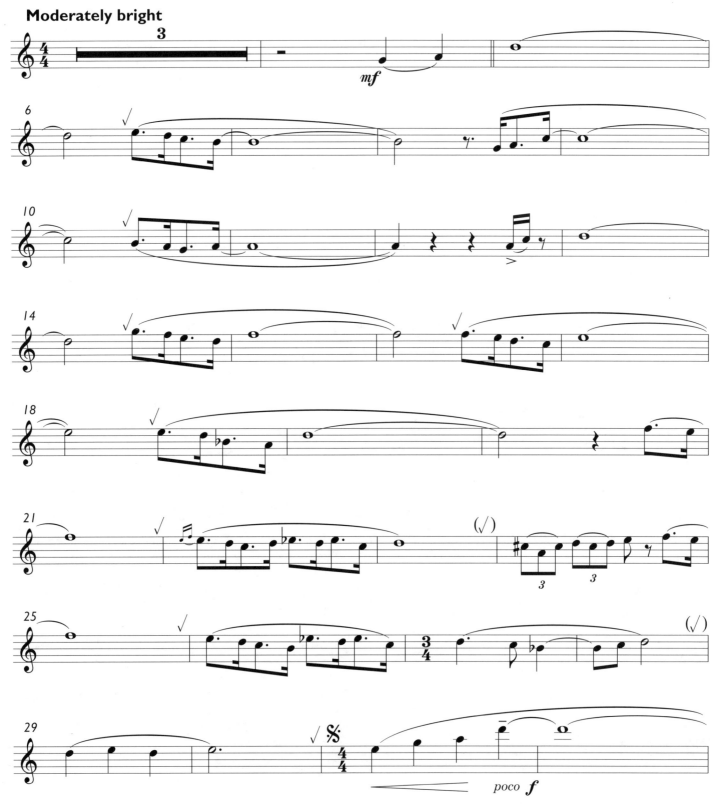

THE ENTERTAINER

By Scott Joplin.

This piano rag featured in the film 'The Sting'. Make sure you keep a very steady tempo.
You will find that the piece is quite a test of stamina.

9/01 (41463)